All Day/All Night ALL WOMAN

All Day/All Night

ALL WOMAN

How to be a SUCCESS as a WOMAN 24 hours a day!

by JEANNIE SAKOL

Charles of the Ritz Group Ltd.

NEW YORK

Charles of the Ritz Group Ltd.
40 West 57th Street
New York, N.Y. 10019

Library of Congress Catalog Card No. 78-60150

ISBN 0-9601800-1-X

First Printing 1978

Designed by Jack Meserole

Printed in the United States of America

Dedicated to

ALL WOMEN

Who as working women,
mothers and wives,
successfully manage
their many-dimensional lives.
Each is equal but different,
and glad to be a woman.
We call her
the 24-Hour Woman.

Contents

PART **III**
**YOU VERSUS
THEM**

Introduction

We at Charles of the Ritz are devoted to the concerns of women for the very good reason that women are the consumers we serve. In this quest we have talked with many thousands of women to find out how they feel about basic values, responsibilities, and their lives in general.

We realized recently that, by sharing what we've learned with *all* women, we could play a positive role in women's special quest for self-fulfillment and success. It's all part of "The Ladies Mafia"! (See Chapter 9.)

SOME BASICS

One major theme emerged in every part of the country: In our hearts we women have not changed; the options from which we choose have simply broadened and multiplied. This is, in fact, the great change that everyone is talking about today.

Words have also changed in interpretation to fit the times. "Femininity" itself has taken on a new meaning. Think of what it used to mean. The old idea of the "feminine" woman was a simpering birdbrain who burst into tears when the toothpaste cap rolled down the drain, a cutie-pie who could barely turn a key in the lock by herself. She accepted her husband's decisions as a duty, her mate's sexual demands as a martyr, and her passive role as inevitable. At one time we were taught to conform to this definition. Later, many women reacted by calling for the "death" of femininity.

It was reassuring when I heard unanimous agreement, from women in all walks of life that femininity is indeed alive and well. It is healthier, happier, and more beautiful than ever. The old interpretation of the word was simply too superficial and vulnerable to obsolescence. The true meaning of femininity runs deep into our innermost feelings. It is our trait, completely intertwined with our identity. It's our special charisma. One woman in Chicago summed it up very well when talking about fragrance: "Actually, I want to feel feminine for myself because that's what's inside me and what is me. I would feel void and naked without it."

Femininity is our gentle strength, our sensitivity to others' feelings, our inner glow. It comes out in our behavior, our personalities, our appearance. And there are as many expressions of femininity as there are individual women.

Femininity coexists perfectly with all of our other personal goals. It is an affirmation of womanhood in all aspects of life. There is no conflict. Nothing is more powerful than strength with gentleness; nothing more right than stepping forward and doing what you think is best, while respecting others at the same time. Today's feminine women are competent, imaginative, loving, and self-reliant. We are doing more with our lives—and enjoying the multi-dimensional challenges of home and career.

Of the country's 80 million women, over half—that's over 40 million of us—work full or part time in addition to our other responsibilities. The cultural heroine of the past was a sheltered love bird in a gilded cage. Today's heroine leads an active, many-faceted life with verve and gusto as a:

- *Homemaker and Mother*, caring for home and children;

- *Wife and Lover*, to her husband;

- *Working Woman*, responsible for her job and income; and

- *Her Own Individual Person*, aware of her own growth and needs.

As ambitious, competent women, we no longer hide our skills or pretend our successes are silly little accidents. Yes, we know we are equal, but certainly not the same. We bring whole new perceptions to our business and our living. We see things through a different set of lenses. This, in fact, may be our secret weapon. Wonder Woman couldn't have kept as many balls in the air, as we sometimes must. Sure, it's hard. Sure, it's full of trauma sometimes. But we are burgeoning with pride. Pride in achievement. Pride in ourselves as women!

It is with this sense of joyful celebration in our femininity that we commissioned Jeannie Sakol to write this book. She is a woman, like us, who has dedicated her writing career to our careers, ambitions, and feelings. Her healthy ability to laugh with life comes through loud and clear. And it is our hope that you will find this offering an exuberant, completely candid exploration of the options, pleasures (and problems) confronting all of us.

Sincerely,

Brenda Harburger
Vice President, New Products
Charles of the Ritz Group Ltd.

PART

CHOICES

CHAPTER 1

You can have your cake and eat it, too

Sigmund Freud once threw up his hands in exasperation, demanding to know, "What do women *want?*"

If the grump of Vienna were alive and clucking today, he would hear millions of women reply—with confidence and exultation—"Everything!"

But what does *everything* mean? To each of us, it's a different combination of aims and possibilities. Brenda, a Florida homemaker, wants to be a Wife, Mother, Student, and Photographer! Having quit college at nineteen to marry and have two children, she is now, at twenty-six, broadening what she calls her "Wife-style."

"I decided that if I really set my mind to it, I could have my cake and eat it. I could have a good marriage. And give my children proper care. And still make time for some courses. And work at my photography."

Without being a super-woman who gets by on two hours' sleep, Brenda simply reorganized her time and found ways to fit everything in. "For instance, I've become a weekly person instead of a daily person. I plan a week's menus, do all my shopping at once—and do most of the week's cooking at one time. Casseroles. Pies. Fresh vegetables scraped and stored in plastic bags. The whole family helps plan and prepare what we're going to eat.

"The two children go to school—and that's when I go to school, too. I'm back at college working for my degree and I love it! As for photography, it's always been a hobby. Recently, I put up a notice in the supermarket, offering my professional services at children's parties. Not only am I building a following, but I can take my children with me when I work."

A more common cake-and-eat-it situation is the married woman with the part-time job. By dividing your life into two compartments, there is both structure and freedom. The structured aspect demands that you fulfill certain responsibilities at a specific time and in a specific way. That is, your life becomes a giant jigsaw in which the pieces must fit precisely, yet each piece is separate.

As one woman explains it, "I feel like I'm a whole woman for the first time in my life. Much as I love my family, I felt stifled by the day-to-day sameness of my domestic routine. Now that I'm in an office, too, I see the problems of the business world—and my home seems like paradise by comparison."

Having it both ways is something that successful men have always understood. Women are slowly but surely learning that like so many man/woman parallels, the goals are equally possible but the paths are different.

Giving up the Perfect Homemaker image is a common problem for the new working woman. As Francie recalls, "I had this picture of myself as Wonder Wife, devoting every minute of the day to making the perfect home for my family. I made all the kids' clothes, the curtains, bedspreads, slipcovers. I ironed my husband's shirts, drove his invalid mother to the shopping center, made special snacks for the weekly stag poker party—how was I going to keep up with all these things when I started back to work?"

What she did was to become, in her own words, the Less Than Perfect Wife. "And you know what, nobody noticed! The children were just as happy in store-boughts, especially the denims. We paid our oldest boy to iron his father's shirts. He figured out a way to do them fast—and beautifully—and earned himself an extra three dollars a week."

She worked out a revolving schedule between her husband, herself, and a neighbor to ferry her mother-in-law to the shopping mall and simplified the poker-night refreshments to cheese and crackers. Because "the guys" complained about missing her culinary surprises, she makes time when she can to provide a special treat.

Bonita, another recent career returnee, had worried that her sex life would suffer when she took a job. "I thought I'd be too exhausted." The reverse was true. "I found that I was taking better care of myself, watching my weight, paying more attention to my appearance. Work stimulated me, improved my self-confidence. And of course that made me more exciting to my husband—and more exciting to myself."

Totally unexpected was the way Tina's children responded to her job. Contrary to her concern that they would feel deserted, they began to treat her "like a person instead of good old Mom." For the first time, there were genuine discussions at the dinner table. "The children seek out my advice and respect my opinions now," she marvels. "I'm still good old Mom, but I guess now they figure that if I'm savvy enough to hold down a job, I must have something on the ball."

You can have your cake and eat it, too, if and when:

- The entire family feels individually responsible and mutually caring so that eventually household chores are interchangeable and accomplished without fuss or bother.

- Work and self-fulfillment are an encouraged part of every family member's life from the tiniest toddler learning to talk to grandparents in retirement.

- Sexual relations become increasingly intimate because of shared respect and responsibility (and income) rather than the neurotic struggles based on financial dependency.

Once you have achieved a genuinely affirmative view of yourself in both the home and the working world, you can confidently have your cake, cut it to taste, and enjoy it at will. Once you're your own woman, you can be every and any woman you wish to be. About the only time you can't have your cake and eat it too is in the literal sense, when you're on a weight-loss diet!

The working couple: you can work it out

It is Ellen's first day as a full-time working wife. The alarm goes off, as usual, at six. She groans theatrically, as usual, and staggers to the kitchen to start breakfast. Returning to the bedroom, she finds the double bed empty, as usual. Skip, as usual, has gone into the bathroom, as usual . . .

"Darling—" she calls through the bathroom door.

"What—"

"Would you mind getting a move on, please?"

For Ellen and Skip, the morning is not "as usual." Ellen is going to work, too. She has to dress, put on makeup, and get her act together. She wants a shower. Skip is taking a shower. She opens the bathroom door. The steam is thick as a milk shake. Skip is singing.

7

What's wrong with him? Does he want her to be late her first day? A hideous suspicion forms in her mind. He is purposely taking his time. He doesn't really want her to go to work.

"Hurry up, dammit!" she shouts.

"Where's my shirt?" he shouts back.

"The bathroom floor is like a river. Who do you think I am, Jacques Cousteau?" she replies.

This is the kind of small Bathroom War that can break out when the wife takes a full-time job. When it first came up, Skip said he was delighted that Ellen had a job. They didn't really *need* the extra money to survive, but like most people they could sure use it to help pay off the mortgage and to have a nicer vacation than last year.

ANXIETY AND CHANGE

Now that the big day has arrived, Ellen can see that Skip is having a severe anxiety attack. His demands on her are his way of seeking reassurance that he is still of prime importance in her life.

On the other hand, the newly working wife should not automatically regard all aspects of the Bathroom War as anxiety. Early morning habits are hard to change. If your husband has always had complete run of the bathroom while you waited until he left for work to get your act together, you could be expecting too much from him. He can't possibly know your morning pattern unless you tell him.

PATIENCE AND PLANNING

It takes a bit of patience and planning, but you can work out the logistics. You may shower at night and let him shower in the morning. You may shower first and then put on the coffee while he showers—or you may shower together, a pleasant way to start the day and save on the water bills, too. As for the bathroom mirror, a small investment puts a separate mirror in the bedroom.

A good occupational skill for the working wife to develop is a third ear for actually hearing her husband's fears, jealousies, anxieties, and resentments however he may disguise them. The husband is traditionally the head of household and provider. Your husband is genuinely proud of your ambition and sincerely wants a partnership marriage with you.

However, be aware that he is probably suffering a good deal of inner turmoil. "What's wrong, can't you support your own wife?" a relative might tease him. Statistics may show that most women are joining the work force. He knows this, yet—he feels less competent.

Also gnawing at his vitals is raw, grinding insecurity. You're attractive. You will be meeting men with more drive, ambition, and success than your husband. Your "hero" feels diminished, his place in your life is threatened. He knows the seductions of the working world—he may have had a fling or two of his own! How can he compete?

Speaking of competition, it may surprise you to know that your husband may start to compete with you.

"With *me?* But I'm earning about half his salary!"

It doesn't matter what you're earning now. He knows how determined you are to get ahead. He sees other women advancing up the success ladder. "I'm going to lose her. She's going to walk out on me!" a tipsy young husband confides to a stranger at a party. "She's smarter than I am. I've always known that. Why couldn't she just stay home and be a wife?"

For a working couple to work it out, much of the initiative must come from the wife. Your husband may feel neglected, deprived, and bewildered. He most certainly will have difficulty expressing his emotions and therefore may not be in the best frame of mind to initiate solutions. Give him a start and give him time.

ANTICIPATE, TOLERATE, CONCILIATE, NEGOTIATE

His world is changing as much as yours. You are no longer the girl he married. You are a woman who works. You are no longer totally dependent on him for support. You are a working partner. You are a threat to his male ego, a challenge to his male pride.

♡ **ANTICIPATE** a period of petulant criticism. There's too much starch in his shirts. The house is a holy mess. Dessert was store-bought instead of homemade. How come there's no beer? Or bulbs? Who used up all the stamps?

♡ **TOLERATE** these small-boy temper tantrums. They are temporary. He's really saying he loves you, he needs you, and how come you're not paying attention to him! (New working wives report a sudden increase in sexual demands. "My husband seems to wait for me to fall asleep before he starts making love.

It's a terrible thought, but I keep thinking he's trying to wear me out so I can't go to work in the morning!")

♡ **CONCILIATE** with him during a brief period of transition, a few weeks or months while he adjusts to your new working life together. If he's having a temper tantrum because you haven't sewn a button on his blazer, don't fight fire with fire. Bite your tongue. Don't inquire if his arm is broken or shout, "What am I, your maid?"

Sew on the button. Bake up a few of his favorite pies and put them in the freezer. Answer his grumps with a smile and a kiss. Respond to his sexual overtures with passion and tenderness. He knows what an oaf he's being and once the rough period is past, he will undoubtedly apologize to you for his behavior. Do those loving little extras for him during the transition period.

By understanding his emotional turmoil, you will ease it. If you respond in kind with anger and sarcasm, you will make things worse by confirming his fears.

"But what about me?" you may well ask. "What about my fears and insecurities on the job? How about my fatigue and guilts about neglecting my husband and my home?" Your patience and caring will be worth the effort.

♡ **NEGOTIATE** a new structure for your marriage, an up-front method for mutual understanding, emotional support, and shared responsibility. Working it out means talking it out.

Your first few weeks of working are crucial—a period of adjustment. Make a list of what these adjustments are:

- Meals.

- Shopping.

- Fatigue.

- Energy.

- Responsibilities in the home.

- Pressures at work.

- Money.

Make time and create the opportunity to sit down alone with your husband and discuss these things—although not all at once!

WHOSE MONEY IS IT?

The most important adjustment will probably be money. What happens to your salary? Will you save the whole thing for a specific project: a summer cottage, a trip to South America, a slush fund for the children's education and orthodontia?

Or, perhaps you will divide the family's financial responsibilities in an agreed-to formula, that is, he pays certain continuing monthly bills—the mortgage, utilities, and car payment; you pay for food, insurance, and entertainment. Both of you may decide to keep separate bank accounts. Whatever you decide to do, be sure you get sound tax advice on whether to file tax returns separately or together.

"But my money is my money!" some new working wives feel. "I'm still doing my homemaker job for free, so why shouldn't my husband continue to pay all the household expenses as before?"

Women who feel this way are being totally unfair. That a woman should feel this way provides a revealing insight into the friction and misunderstandings in many marriages. The reason to offer to share your salary is that he has always shared his. If you have other plans for the money—and sound reasons for them—

discuss the matter with your husband. Don't spring it on him as if he's not involved.

For the wife entering the job market for the first time, there will be a sudden understanding of what her breadwinner husband has known all the time. It takes time, it takes energy, it takes skill and hard work to earn money. Having experienced this, you will gain new perceptions about money, how to handle it, and how to use it wisely.

CHORES: WHO DOES WHAT?

Another adjustment is taking care of your home. Simplify household chores. Make up a list of all the things that must be done to run a comfortable home: Meals. Laundry. Upkeep. Maintenance. Avoid "putting an apron" on your husband. If he really feels a woman's place is in the kitchen, give him time to adjust. Approach the division of labors something like this:

You will cook the meals and see that the kitchen is well stocked.

He will do the floors; you will do the dusting.

He will agree to mop up the bathroom; you will keep your makeup shelves and other grooming aides neat.

If you sleep in a big double bed, you will make it together (in about ten seconds flat).

You will also do your supermarket shopping together once a week with a list you've made out together. This way, it's a joint responsibility to see that the household does not run out of toilet paper, soap, razor blades, *or* that garlicky salami you both love!

♡ **FEARS AND RESENTMENTS** You should encourage him to express his fears and resentments and you express yours. A Con-

necticut couple sets aside Saturday morning for their Private
Time together. He puts off his golf or tennis until the afternoon.
She changed her ceramics course to the same afternoon.

"We sleep until we wake up and then we usually make love
and then make breakfast on a wheel cart and get back into bed to
eat and drink coffee and talk about what's bothering us."

One Saturday morning, this couple worked out a potentially
destructive problem. He had invited four people to dinner
without asking her or offering to help. Instead of getting angry,
she said, "I'm flattered that you think I'm Super-woman." Instead
of complaining, "You never lift a finger when we have company."
She firmly asked, "why don't you make the salad while I prepare
the quiche?"

Don't demean him; involve him. When the guests arrive, don't
make jokes at his expense. If they compliment the food or the
table setting, let him decide whether or not he wants to take a
bow for his efforts. Let him reply. Don't answer for him.

SHOE ON THE OTHER FOOT

A more difficult problem was a business trip that she was going to make. Her company's annual sales meeting would entail a
four-day weekend at a Caribbean hotel. "I was so thrilled at the
idea, I didn't realize that he would feel threatened. At first, I was
going to say, 'So what—you're a big boy, you go on business trips,
why can't I?' "

Instead, she immediately verbalized all the resentments she
knew he must be feeling. "You probably feel I'm deserting you.
That I'd rather be with my company in the Caribbean than with

you. That somebody might seduce me. That I don't care what happens to you on Saturday night. Well, you're wrong. I do care about you. And I also care about me."

She then listened while he poured out his feelings. How he would feel like an idiot at the Saturday night get-together with their friends. How he wanted to be the one to walk on a moonlit beach with her—not some water-cooler Romeo.

The discussion was not about whether or not she would go. That was decided. What they were doing was working out and airing their innermost feelings. When he finished, it was again her turn to say that the trip was important to her. It meant the company had confidence in her abilities. It distressed her that he was unhappy. She told him how important his encouragement was. She told him of her love and need for him.

And when she was away, she called him every night at bedtime . . . just as she likes him to do when he's away. Despite her busy schedule, she found the time to buy him a personal gift, something special to make her homecoming a celebration for them both. Nor did she spoil the reunion by overwhelming him with the fun and triumphs of her trip.

Most of all, she gave him a lot of "I love you's" both long distance and short-nightied before and after the separation.

GUILT AND FATIGUE

Two other areas that concern the working couple are guilt and fatigue. After centuries of cultural conditioning, even the most emancipated woman feels a pang of guilt about "neglecting" her wifely responsibility. It may sound cruel, but many household chores are unnecessary make-work. A little dust never hurt anyone. Paper plates are fine for breakfast or snack meals. A once-a-month professional housecleaning is worth the money. So is one of those magic machines that make juice, puree, pastry, or anything else in a flash.

Guilt is self-serving sentimentality. It uses up energy and makes for premature wrinkles. It is also as boring to other people as it is to you. The world's top guaranteed conversation stopper begins, "Oh, I feel so guilty —"

This especially pertains to sex. If working makes you "too tired" to make love, it's time to examine your true relationship with your husband. If this "problem" persists, it might be that you have subconsciously been "paying" for his financial support with your sexual favors, as they say in Washington. Now earning your own money, you may psychologically be feeling you're paying your way in cash.

On the other hand, sexual languor may simply be fatigue. A full-time job is emotionally as well as physically exhausting. When you get home, you may have nothing left to give.

♡ **QUIET COLLAPSE** Many working women are solving this problem with an After Work Collapse. Even those with children find that it works wonders. As one explained, "I have made it a household rule. The hour between six and seven at night is mine. I am not to be disturbed unless the house is burning down. I take off my clothes, get into bed with the lights off and some soft music on. I breathe deeply and empty my mind. I may fall asleep or just rest. If Ed [her husband] wants to join me, he's welcome as long as he doesn't talk."

When she emerges at seven, she is full of energy and enthusiasm. The evening ahead is a joy instead of a drag.

P.S. Joe has also discovered that a Quiet Hour at home with

his wife does more to relax him than a Happy Hour of drinking at the cocktail bar near his office.

Each working couple is different, of course. By working it out on your own, your marriage promises to be stronger, happier, and more rewarding than ever.

Working . . .
with children

There are three kinds of Working Mothers.

The One-Income Mother who is the sole support of her family. For her, there's no choice. If she doesn't work, they don't eat.

The Shared-Income Mother whose earnings combine with her husband's to provide a well-rounded life-style. If she doesn't work, they don't have orthodontia, a piano, or college.

The Extra-Income Mother whose earnings provide investments for real estate, trust funds, and the like. Since she is not severely pressed for money, this mother may embark on a career that doesn't pay too much at the start but may have a lucrative future. If she doesn't work, her children may not be deprived of things money can buy them, but they may be stuck with a bored mother.

Whatever her need or motivation, every working mother's fundamental concern is her children. However, her work emphasizes her desire to grow and prosper as a woman while at the same time giving her children the love, attention, and direction they should have in order to grow up to be strong, functioning adults.

"How will my working affect my children?" is a constantly nagging refrain. In the back of every working woman's mind is a TV image of runaway girls who become speed freaks and prostitutes and sullen adolescent boys jailed for armed robbery or in psycho wards—because the mother wasn't on hand after school with the milk and marshmallow cookies.

Whether to work or not to work is not the subject of this chapter. That's for each woman to decide on the basis of economic and intellectual necessity. Since working is very much a "fact of wife" in so many families, the question is how does the working mother give her youngsters a good childhood on which to build a happy, productive life?

♡ **QUALITY VS. QUANTITY**   Experts agree that the quality of mothering can be more important than the quantity of time spent with children. A typical experience is Merri's. "I never used to get dressed in the morning. My two little boys would come home from nursery school for lunch and the breakfast dishes would still be on the table, the house a mess, me in a bad temper. I knew I had the whole day to get my act together, so I'd never really get going until the afternoon.

"I'd give them their lunch. I didn't have much to say to them. They couldn't wait to get outside and play. I could have been a machine for all the communicating we did."

Advised to get a job because of her depression, Merri is now up early each morning. "I've got things to do, places to go!" She and the boys roughhouse and have fun while she gets them ready for school. They "help" her pack their lunch, while the whole family, including Dad, have breakfast. A sitter takes care of them in the afternoon, taking them places and teaching them sports. When Merri gets home at six, the boys are bursting with things to tell her.

"I'm much more of a person working. They sense it and respond," she reports. "I feel better, look better, and have more to give them, and they can sense that. And P.S., I have a cleaning service — the dishes are washed and the house is neat."

A young advertising manager advises, "The working mother should put the emphasis on *mother*." You can be a vice-president of the company but to your children, you are first of all their Mom. They must know where and how to find you at all times with the understanding that your place of work is like your bedroom, its privacy is respected except for emergency.

"I phone my children once a day when they get home from school. If they're going somewhere else, they have permission to call me. Conversation is short and sweet. How are they? Do they feel okay? Did anything great happen? Let's save it to discuss at dinner. Sometimes, I ask what they want for dessert. Just to make things fun, I occasionally announce I'm bringing home a surprise."

In discussing the subject with a cross-section of working mothers, here are:

TEN TERRIFIC TIPS ON BEING A SUCCESSFUL WORKING MOTHER

1. *Hugs and Kisses* . . . like chocolate chips in cookies and fried onions, there can never ever be enough demon-

stration of affection and caring. Little boys love it as much as little girls, by the way, and will grow up less inhibited about showing affection than previous male generations. One mother says she puts a single chocolate kiss in each child's lunch as an "extra" kiss while she's at work.

2. *Listening and Remembering* . . . tune out your job; tune in your child and really listen! If a few days later, your little girl mentions something you don't remember, she'll know you weren't hearing what she said and her trust in you will suffer. Remember promises, too; your child does. If you've promised a treat or an excursion to playland or a skating rink, and find you can't make it, don't think that if you don't mention it the child will have forgotten. Children's minds are like little computer imprints. Tell the child how disappointed you are and you know how disappointed she or he is — and make a new date.

3. *Make Them Proud of Mommy's Career* . . . if possible, have your children pick you up at work (the sitter or grandparent can bring them) unless regulations forbid it. Show them where you work, where you sit, and what you do. This can be very exciting for a child and give him or her something to brag about at school and on the playground.

4. *Consistency* . . . always be with them at dinnertime and bedtime so they can count on your presence. If a business trip or a heavy schedule of working late is on the horizon, give them plenty of warning: "I'm going to be away for two days next week." . . . "I have a big conference to get ready for, so I'm going to be working late at the office next week." Little children who don't quite know what these things mean will enjoy reporting these events to their playmates ("My Mommy's out of town; yours is not!")

5. *Always Be on Hand for Special Events* . . . parents' night, the school play, the class picnic, a mother's place is in the audience. There are not that many of these special events and usually they are at night. For the rare afternoon event, you have plenty of time in which to request a few hours off.

6. *Magic Times Together* . . . establish a routine of special shared times. A mother of three girls has a "Beauty Parlor" night once a week when she trims their nails, gives them a special shampoo, sticks them under her own drier, and lets them hang around while she sees to her own grooming routine. "They love being included in!" Another mother makes Sunday breakfast a private time for the children and her husband, the children deciding the menu and helping to prepare it. As her children's interest in the outdoors grew, one mother met the challenge by learning to ski and scuba dive in order to join the fun on family excursions.

7. *Reassure Them About Emergencies* . . . even the full-time mother is not always right there when Janie falls off a swing or Bill's appendix starts to explode. Ironically, the working mother is sometimes easier to find than the homemaker who might be at the supermarket or running an errand when trouble strikes. Make sure each child has your business number (and your husband's) with them — in a locket around the neck, on a card slipped in with their bus pass. Make sure they know that their school and baby-sitter can reach you at a moment's notice.

8. *Write Them Notes* . . . as young children learn to write, what more exciting means of using this new skill than to have a daily correspondence with their mother and father?

This encourages children to express themselves, and you'll have a chance to see what's on their minds. Moreover, it's exciting and fun to leave little notes for other people—and to get them!

9. *Don't Apologize for Going to Work* . . . to do so suggests that you are doing something bad to them. They may wonder what they did wrong to be "punished" and feel ashamed instead of proud of your career.

10. *Guard Against Being Jealous of Sitters and Teachers* . . . it's healthy for children to relate to adults other than you and your husband. Never indicate any sign of jealousy when your children say they "love" Mary Ellen or Ms. Mason at school. Occasionally a child will reach for the sitter's hand, automatically saying "Mommy," which may make your heart sink for a moment, but don't put your youngsters on the spot by asking, "Do you like her more than you like me?" or anything else that divides loyalties. Be glad your child is affectionate and responsive to other adults—that's a sure sign you are a good mother!

CHAPTER 4

Independent endeavors

Maybe it's time to wage a small war of independence. Maybe the moment is ripe to declare a state of independence and create a small but separate country. An undeveloped country to explore and build into something uniquely and solely yours.

Independent endeavors are the things that you must do for yourself. Nobody can buy them for you or give them to you. They are yours for the seeking and the getting. The choice is a wide one. Life is a giant pastry board. It's up to you to choose and to discover whether your choice was a good one.

Some choices seem extremely tempting from a distance. "I'd love to play the piano," says Sheila. But after three lessons, she was unwilling to practice and uncertain about renting a piano.

"If I hadn't married so young, I'd have been an artist," says Gail. She buys brushes, oils, canvas, an easel and stares at them for three weeks before stashing them in the garage with the mandolin and tie-dye equipment.

24

Politics fascinate Peggy. Attractive, persuasive, and much liked in her community, she joins her local political party thinking that in no time at all she will be a mover and shaker and maybe even a candidate for public office. After a few months of typing envelopes, manning the clubhouse phones, and sitting through speeches that put her to sleep, she retired from public service.

When pursuing an independent endeavor, there are two things to keep in mind. You must want it a lot and you must commit yourself to achieve your goal.

The choice being yours, here are some possibilities to consider.

RUN AWAY FROM HOME

This is not a recommendation to disappear after breakfast one day, leaving your family to beat the bushes for your mutilated body. The time might simply be right for you to take a sabbatical from your life. The heavily married woman will say, "I'd love to, but what about my family?"

To answer a question with a question: What if you broke your leg and were laid up for a month or so? They would get along without you and look forward to your return. What's more, if you were to plan a runaway, things could be prepared to go a lot more smoothly than if an accident did suddenly put you out of commission.

The critical question, of course, is what or where would you run away to? This is an opportunity to explore your own independence in a practical way, to discover that you can get along without your family if need be. By testing your own independence, you strengthen your relationships with members of your family and find out new things about yourself.

A runaway adventure might be:

- A short trip alone (how long since you've gone anywhere alone?) to see an old friend or attend a festival you've read about and dreamed of seeing or simply to go with the flow, taking what comes as it comes.

- Work on a farm or at a country inn among people and a life-style utterly different from yours—a good way to get perspective and also to just enjoy a complete change of pace for a few weeks. All it takes is a list of local inns.

- Give in to a persistent whim. Return to the place you were born and trace back your roots. Or take a cheap package trip to London and go to the theater every night.

START YOUR OWN BUSINESS

Perhaps the most independent endeavor to try, your own business, should be approached as a *business*, not a hobby. If you're going to cater private parties, find out about such things as cost and overhead. Otherwise, you'll find yourself charging ten dollars a head while the food and labor add up to twice that amount.

A survey of successful small one-woman operations have one thing in common. The business revolves on one product or one specific service. A Santa Monica woman specializes in cold soups: vichyssoise, gazpacho, and borscht. She accepts telephone orders only, twenty-four hours in advance, and a minimum order of two gallons. Her soups are delicious. She knows ahead of time how much to prepare and what arrangements to make for delivery. She has a station wagon fitted up with a refrigerator. Customers have suggested she expand her menu. At the moment, she can't. If business continues good, she may have to move her business out of her home and into a larger kitchen — which means overhead and other expenses that may not be worth the trouble.

A one-product or single-service business might be:

♡ **TUTOR** If you've kept up or boned up on your college major, there's no reason you can't give private tutoring in English, French, history, math, music appreciation, religion.

Check out the local hourly rate for private tutoring. Put up a notice in churches, schools, and the community center: "REMEDIAL READING & WRITING. Private tutoring in high-school reading and comprehension. Instruction in writing themes and composition. Phone . . ." Helping someone to learn — especially a young person — is gratifying to the heart and refreshing to the intellect. And it puts money in the bank.

♡ **TELEPHONE MESSAGE SERVICE** Have an extra telephone installed. Take a small ad and have some cards printed offering to take messages for people for a monthly fee. Traveling salesmen and other people with small businesses who don't want to use their home phones depend on this kind of service.

♡ **OTHERS** A painter who specializes in animal portraits. A blonde, brunette, and red-haired car-washing team who custom-wash your car and simonize it in your own driveway. A rural Pennsylvania woman who travels to Philadelphia once a month and does errands for her neighbors for a small "carrying charge."

For free expert advice on starting your own business, how to keep records, pay bills, and otherwise run things professionally, consult the federal Small Business Administration, listed in your local telephone directory under United States Government *or* simply write to them in Washington, D.C.

CHANGE YOUR APPEARANCE

To lose twenty pounds is to make yourself independent of your destructive eating habits.

To learn about nutrition and makeup is to make you independent of anxiety and doubts about your personal appeal.

To make running or swimming an integral part of your daily regimen is to declare your body independent and free to grow strong and resistant to disease.

How to know if you're making the right choice?

As discussed earlier, nobody can buy an independent endeavor for you or give it to you for your birthday. Only you can take advantage of opportunities close at hand and take the first step. Only you can make a choice and only you know if it's the right one.

CHAPTER 5

Live alone and love it: the New Cave Woman

People who live in high-rise apartments are often called cave dwellers. In recent years, a new species of cave dweller has developed. She is the woman who lives alone and loves it, the New Cave Woman.

Divorced, widowed, or simply single, she has many things in common with her primitive ancestors. She has developed a keen sense of survival and a highly developed set of skills for doing it in style.

The New Cave Woman makes her cave warm, cozy, and safe from intruders—unless she specifically invites one in. Her cave is her base from which she goes foraging for food and furs and an occasional "cave" drawing to hang on the wall. If she sees a friendly maverick male of the species wandering around loose, she might capture him and drag him back to the cave, leaving until later the decision of whether or not to keep him as a permanent trophy or merely as a warm companion on a cold night.

The choice of becoming a New Cave Woman is increasingly open to the contemporary woman. With divorce statistics at an all-time high and going higher and with many young women choosing not to marry straight out of school, there is every possibility that you may be living at least part of your life without a permanent man.

The image of a woman living alone has often been a pathetic one. Generally presumed to be neurotic, sex-starved, and desperate, she was generally portrayed as having a pimple on her nose, a drinking habit, and no friends, male or female, except for a saintly cousin who invited her to Sunday dinner out of pity.

Unless she could "trap" a man, "land" a husband, or move in with her family as a glorified servant, baby-sitter, or Good Old Aunt Mary, there was little choice except for her to be grim and bear it.

The last decade has made living alone an exciting option. It may be temporary, the period before or between marriages. It could turn out to be permanent, more and more by choice. Above all, it can be an affirmative and growing experience that is gratifying in itself and good survival training for whatever your future life holds.

"I love living alone!" a New Cave Woman recently stated. Divorced after eight years of marriage, Felice confessed, "I love having my bed all to myself and reading as late as I like without somebody turning off the light. I love going to work and having a sandwich for dinner if that's what I want, and no apologies. I love spreading a dress pattern on the floor without being in anyone's way. I love handling my own affairs, spending my money as I see fit, and learning to manage from my own mistakes."

Wendy, another New Cave Woman, has not married. Two years out of college, she had been sharing an apartment with two former college roommates. "It suddenly hit me that I'd never lived by myself. I went from my parents' home to college and then carried the dorm life to the apartment. We were working, but it was still like being in school."

Her cave is a large, sunny studio in a Minneapolis apartment complex. Bright and ambitious, she is a systems analyst. "My job is very demanding. I spend three or four nights a week alone at home, resting and preparing for the next day. I don't want anyone in my hair or to deal with problems other than my own. The other nights I can present myself at my most charming, well-dressed, well-rested, friendly best as I date, see friends, or entertain at home. Weekends are for sports, tennis in summer, skiing in winter.

"Living alone gives me total control over how I use my time and energies. I want to succeed. If I fail, I have only myself to blame. That's why—however I'm tempted—my 'in' times are really 'in' so that when I'm out for a wonderful time, I'm sure to be at my best."

Just so you don't think she's entirely self-engrossed, she gives six hours a week to volunteer work at a nearby hospital and is known among her friends as a considerate and thoughtful person who's "always there when you need her."

As you can see, work is basic to the New Cave Woman. She is responsible for her income, and this income enables her to live, learn, and love as she feels is best for her.

But, you may ask, what about that warm companion mentioned earlier? Does the New Cave Woman go out marauding with a club, bringing her subdued prey home like a piece of meat much the way Cave Men have always done? Is primitive sex all that interests the New Cave Woman? What about tenderness and friendship with men?

According to anthropologists, females of most species are the nesters, the nurturers. The human species is no exception. Marlene Dietrich scrubs floors and baby-sits for her grandchildren. Elizabeth Taylor puts up family pictures wherever she travels. Helen Gurley Brown makes a low-calorie salad seem like a feast.

The woman who succeeds in a man's world can do so by recognizing that men and women are equal but different—and never more so than in personal relations. At a certain moment, the New Cave Woman will find that the male beast she has captured is actually a domestic animal worth hanging on to. At which point, she'll have to make a decision; to clean out the closets or to move to a bigger cave.

CHAPTER

Sexual freedom: you can say no

You're divorced or separated and just getting back into the social madness known as dating. You've just come home from a first evening out with a new man. It's good-bye time at the old front door. "I had a great time," you say.

"You mean you're throwing me out?" He looks as if he has been hit with a spear.

"I hope we see each other again," you continue and to make it clear that you mean it, you add, "Come to dinner next Tuesday," meaning you're willing to spring for a meal, too.

"You mean you're throwing me out?" Apoplexy. Rage. Sneer. "What's the *matter* with you," he demands.

There's nothing the matter with you. Yes, he did buy you dinner, but you are not on the menu as dessert. Yes, you've made love with other men and have every intention of doing it again. With style and enthusiasm. But with whom and under what

33

impulse or circumstances is entirely up to you—no explanations or apologies required.

Women's sexual freedom is gravely misunderstood by many men. The freedom is actually twofold. Civilization has progressed to the point of giving us freedom to choose mates and lovers according to our own values and emotions. Education and contraception have given us freedom from fear of pregnancy and venereal disease.

Too many men—especially those who think from the waist down—tend to emphasize the first syllable, *free,* leaving unspoken the last syllable, which becomes an ironic comment on their dim perception, *dumb.*

Sexual freedom does not mean sex on demand. That is not freedom but another form of sexual tyranny. Further, the practical considerations are horrendous. If you slept with everyone who said, "Hey, Baby, let's go!" you'd suffer from bodily exhaustion and dulled senses.

Most of us have grown up in a society in which a woman is either *good* or *bad* and either says "Yes" or "No." It is the basis of considerable misunderstanding. The male vocabulary is still distressingly riddled with expressions of sexual exploitation. You'll hear a man talk about *scoring, hustling* a *chick, babe, cutie* or *honey.* Repellent and pathetic at the same time, many men still "operate" on the basis of dinner as a trade deal and sex as part of the package.

Illogical it may be, but there persists the assumption that a woman's virginity is like a bottle of champagne. Once the cork has been popped, *whoopee,* the party's on, everyone line up.

"You do it for other guys, why not me?"

The point is, you don't do it *for* just any guy. You make love *with* a man you want. As one newly divorced New Yorker observed dryly, "I'm not a service station—or a knothole in a fence or a health club or one of those late-night deposits so cherished by banks."

However many men you may have known, a First Time is still a historic First. It is a new voyage of discovery with its own special innocence that is made more special because of the added pride and confidence that come from having known other faces and other rooms.

To enjoy sexual freedom, you must insist on your own terms; the experience should ennoble you and allow you to respect sexual expression as a gift of nature to be savored rather than squandered.

"I'm just a girl who can say no!" might be a good personal creed. Though you can say Yes with delight, you can equally, rightfully say No, because you're free.

Free to choose.

PART

CLOSE ENCOUNTERS
OF ALL KINDS

CHAPTER 7

Men: the ABC's of loving

Love is a many-splintered thing, a close encounter of the most varied kind. It can range from warm affection to molten passion and applies to everything from a volcanic moment of madness to a shared lifetime of experience and growth.

You will love many men in your life, husbands and otherwise. Each close encounter will be different. Each man will have something special to give you and will also demand special things from you in return.

You may find yourself playing a variety of roles. Depending on the man, the situation, and your particular feelings for him, you may be a geisha girl, a den mother, a sex therapist, a good pal, a best friend, a chief cook — or any combination thereof.

The one constant in all close encounters is that you care about the man and that you are both willing and able to show it. "But if I show my feelings, won't I be vulnerable?" you may ask. Everyone is vulnerable; by showing your feelings, you become open to *his* feelings and therefore able to deepen the relationships with all the men in your life.

Here is a general vocabulary for expressing love in all your close encounters with men, married or not.

A

aggressive affection   To be the object of his affections, make him the subject of yours.

applesauce   The flattery that gets you somewhere, the loving appreciation for his efforts, his success, his thoughtfulness, his appearance.

B

bed manners   The etiquette of courtesy and consideration for your partner however X-rated your bedtime story may be.

breakfast   Have it together even if it means getting up a few minutes earlier.

C

closet   Be sure he has one all to himself.

cushions   There can never be enough for catnapping, cuddling, and making a cozy bed on the floor.

D

dance   An impromptu belly-dance solo calculated to turn him into Zorba or a feverish Saturday-night disco duet at home, making your own colored lights explode.

diplomacy   The best way to maintain friendly relations and prevent explosive skirmishes.

E

eggs   The universal symbol of life and love; learn to fix them exactly as he likes them, or let him fix his own—no matter how he leaves the pan.

ears   Whisper sweet somethings into his at frequent intervals.

F

familiarity   Breeds content.

flirting   Husband or lover, he's still a man.

flowers   There's no rule against sending a man some posies and a note to remind him, "I'm thinking of you."

G

gift   Unexpected.

grapes   Ice cold seedless and served in bed.

grief   Shared and unashamed.

H

hair (yours)   Wiped out of the sink, brushed simply for bed (and never in rollers).

hair (his)   Admired if thick, ignored if thin, compared to Kojak if applicable.

hugs   Frequent, fervent but never as a preliminary to asking a favor.

I

ice cream   In bed to cool you down after making love.

imagination   Taking the routine out of the routine.

intuition   Keeping tuned to his frequency so you "hear" at once when his battery is running down.

J

jealousy   File it and forget it.
jokes   Plenty, shared but never at his expense.

K

ketchup   The proven male tranquilizer and aphrodisiac.
kindness   The cement that strengthens your relationship.
kisses   "A kiss in time saves whine."

L

laughter   People who giggle together wriggle together.
love songs   Get him to sing his favorite lyrics to you; it's a good
   way to break down his inhibitions about love talk.
lucky   Tell him that's how you feel about loving him.

M

memories   Remembrances of flings past kept alive to remind
   you both of how your love has grown.
magazine   Don't read it while he's trying to talk to you.
mutual admiration   The society of lovers.

N

neck   (*noun*) Remember it's part of your face; blend your
   makeup foundation downward to prevent a sudden
   demarkation; (*verb*) even with sexual sophistication, cuddling
   is still one of the finer acts of love.
newspaper   Why fight; get two.

O

oral sex   Open your mouth and say "I love you."
orange   Peel and section one for him as a gesture of intimacy.

P

picnic Get away from it all; mountains, shore, or the bedroom floor.

phone Don't call him more than once a day at work (unless there's an emergency); never answer the phone while making love.

praise Pay close attention to what he does and admire his efforts whether he's painted a bookshelf or come home with a raise; men don't like being taken for granted.

Q

quarrel Yes, when it's necessary to clear the air; no, when it becomes the only means of communication or hotting-up fake excitement.

R

red chiffon nightie For celebrating the special occasion or for making the ordinary occasion special.

reach out If he's silent and withdrawn, don't you be, too; break through the barrier he's erected; he needs help.

S

sarcasm Swallow it, don't let it slip out; save the cutting words for your enemies—your lover is your friend.

sex The best kind is a combination of passion, trust, and generosity of spirit plus a good sense of humor to deal with the silly side.

snoring Don't sleep in the bathtub; sew a gizmo on the back of his pajama top to make him sleep on his stomach (if he sleeps nude, tape a thick wad of cotton to his bare back, just enough to make him turn over).

secrets Keep his no matter what the provocation; they are a sacred trust and must never be used as a weapon unless you want to kill the love.

T

talking things over The first step in solving problems is to discuss them.

tenderness The sweetest gift of love because it benefits both the one who gives and the one who receives.

thanks The best way to show you take nothing for granted.

U

underwear Lots of lace, lots of laundering, lots of changes.

ultimatum Don't give it unless you're prepared to take the consequences; if you put him on the spot, he might X it.

V

valentine Send him one in July.

vacuum cleaner A surefire way to drive him out of the house if you do it while he's reading or watching the game; a dirty floor beats a dirty look any time.

W

whisper Something sexy as he leaves for an important meeting (getting a bank loan, fishing with the guys, asking for that promotion).

worries Share them and solve them together.

X

xylophone A vital word for lovers—of crossword puzzles!

Y

yield   Sometimes on love's winding road, it's better to give in and let him lead the way to your chosen destination — and try not to blind him by flashing your lights from behind.

yesterday   Living today at its fullest so you can look back with satisfaction tomorrow.

Z

zip   Of course you can do it yourself but why not add a touch of intimacy by asking him to zip you in — or *out* — of your clothes.

zoo   Hand-holding and hot dogs, a lunchtime honeymoon.

Hairdresser, doctor, repairman . . .

(or — how to be a Tough Customer!)

One woman whose life seems to run more smoothly than most calls them her stable. "Hairdresser . . . doctor . . . repairman — they don't know it, of course, but I think of them all as stallions I have to train and keep in check to do *my* bidding — instead of the other way around."

Since most of us have grown up with a timid reverence for the men who magically repair bodies and machines, it's hard to view them merely as trained professionals whose job is to provide a needed service. Harder still is to change from being a Helpless Hannah to a Tough Customer.

HAIRDRESSERS

As every woman knows, the biggest challenge is the hairdresser. Especially at a fancy salon, the atmosphere is one of calculated intimidation. They take away your clothes and dress you in a prison gown, demoting you to non-person status.

The stylist, Mr. Tantrum, is prettier than you and a volcano of Oscar performance emotions. Gingerly *touching* your hair as if it were worms, he groans with nauseated disbelief while agonizing over what — if anything — even his genius can do for poor, blighted, hopeless (worthless) you!

The main thing is not to play his game. His job is to take care of your hair. Your job is to get what you want — and for which you are paying.

NEVER, never, *nevaire* say, "I'll leave it up to you. Do what you think is best." That's like making a blind date with Jack the Ripper. You're asking to be zapped and when you emerge hours and dollars later looking like a depraved squirrel, you have no comeback except to invest in some turbans until it all grows out.

In your close encounters with the hairdresser, there's more at stake than the washing machine or wheel alignment. Your job is a delicate one. You must enlist the interest and respect of the technicians (okay, *artistes*) you are paying to enhance your appearance. Just as it's a terrible mistake to turn over the design and decorating of your house to total strangers, it's asking for trouble to abdicate all responsibility for your hair. You're the one who will live in the house; you're the one who will be wearing the hair.

For your next encounter with Monsieur the Magnifique, be utterly prepared.

Bring with you:

Pictures of the new hairstyle you believe will look good on you. Be sure it's plausible and possible. A halo of frizzies is hard to achieve with baby-silk locks—unless you're game for a permanent.

Pictures of yourself in a previous hairstyle that you like, which provides clues on how your hair behaves.

Any special shampoo, conditioners, setting lotions, and so on that work well on your hair. The salon may charge you for applying them (which is fair since they have labor costs), but you have the assurance that the products will work well for you.

Do not be intimidated by:

"Your hair is dry. You should have a treatment." If you don't think it's dry, say so, or play their game with a sweet, "Perhaps next time." If you would like a treatment, ask how much it is beforehand so you won't be surprised at the final tally.

"All the models are wearing short hair." If you haven't had short hair in ages, don't take the plunge until you first try on a short wig and look at yourself ruthlessly in a three-way mirror.

"You'll look ten years younger." Don't grin with joyful expectation. The motive of such a remark is to make you insecure about your age and grateful for whatever is done. Don't conspire to your own humiliation. Don't let him think for even one second that you're being taken in. "Let's save that for another time. Meanwhile, let's concentrate on my hair."

DOCTORS

"Doctors," according to a woman of experience, "are hairdressers with a medical degree." Not quite, perhaps, but the same techniques of intimidation are used to make the seeker of health feel powerless. A leading "woman's complaint" is the old rush act.

The waiting room looks like Macy's on Christmas Eve. An officious assistant keeps assuring all that doctor will be with us shortly. Finally, the great moment arrives. Right? You enter the sanctum sanctorum all primed to connect with your link to health and happiness—only to find him on the phone. And what is he talking about—nuclear medicine? More likely, he's arguing with his wife. Or making a golf date.

You, clearly, are an intrusion. Worse yet, when he does turn his stethoscope in your direction, he makes you feel ashamed of your body and that your ills, aches, and fears are pretty dull stuff. If only you could dazzle him with bubonic plague or a kneecap pregnancy (from having a sexy man sit on your lap). Instead, you mutter, go blank, and meekly allow him to do a cursory examination and write out a few hundred bucks' worth of Rx with no explanation.

And whose fault is all this?

(Chorus): My own fault!

You can save yourself frustration—and enjoy better doctor care—by doing the following:

1. Dress carefully (unless you're leaking at the seams, of course) for your appointment. Be well groomed and made up. This will give you the presence and authority that commands respect, which you won't get if you jump into tacky jeans and a worn t-shirt "just" to run to the doctor's.

2. Write down a list of the things you wish to discuss: symptoms you've been experiencing; the progress of an ongoing condition or treatment; questions about medi-

cines, side reactions—anything and everything you always want to know but forget to ask. Don't be ashamed to take the list out and refer to it. You mean business. The visit is costing you money. You have the right to ask and to get answers.

3. Have a pad handy and write down what he says. If he talks too fast, courteously ask him to repeat or simplify his instructions. As for instance, if you're to take three tablets in the morning, does this mean on awakening, before breakfast, with breakfast, after breakfast, or *instead* of breakfast?

4. If your doctor truly has poor habits such as taking non-emergency phone calls during your consultation, calmly confront him with your feelings. Do not apologize, whine, or make a joke of it. Look him straight in the eyes and say, "You may not realize it, but you're treating me as if I'm not here." Doubtless he will protest or perhaps respond angrily. You continue, if necessary, to point out, "I have come here on a professional call and I expect professional treatment."

♡ **WRITE YOUR OWN SCENARIO**   Yes, doctors tend to treat women like birdbrains. Maybe we've asked for it. Maybe we've been apologetic when something goes wrong with our bodies. Aches, pains, and fatigue in women have long been regarded "neurotic," whereas the same symptoms in men are seen as cause for genuine concern.

In your close encounter with a doctor, have your scenario prepared and rehearsed. It's about time we stop saying, "It's probably nothing . . ." or "Maybe I'm imagining it . . ." or "I hate to take up your time with this . . ." The fact that you've made the appointment, weathered the waiting room, developed your scenario, is proof that you have valid reason to be there.

Repeat, no apologies. Instead, clearly describe your symptoms, that is, "I feel dizzy when I wake up in the morning." . . ."My right leg feels numb after I play tennis." . . . "I keep having stomach cramps with no apparent cause." . . . No little-girl coyness about your "bad" habits; this sounds like *baby bird* begging *daddy's* forgiveness.

A common doctor/patient scene is when he gives you a shot or a prescription (or both). Here, for your interpretation, is a practical scenario.

You: What's in it?

Doctor: Never you mind your pretty little head about that. I'm the doctor.

You: And I'm the patient.

Doctor: Don't you trust me?

You: I'd trust you more if you would tell me what you're giving me.

When he sees you want to be treated as an adult, he will do so. If he doesn't, find another doctor who will.

REPAIRMEN

Use the same tactics during close encounters with other professional men in your life—the plumber, garage mechanic, repairman. Their job is to serve your needs—and your job is to know clearly what your needs are and to get what you're paying for.

There's a gem of sage wisdom that goes: If someone takes advantage of me the first time, it's not my fault. The second time, it is!

To avoid being a pushover, you must erase every last sign of vulnerability in your manner. The "please, you big strong man help poor little baby buttercup me" may possibly get results if you're five feet of whipped cream and cuter'n a bug's ear. Unfortunately, a show of weakness generally leads to getting royally skewered.

♡ **PLUMBERS & CO.**   With the plumber or other repairman coming to your house, generally when you are alone, your comportment should be strictly (and charmingly) business. If you wear an Ann-Margret bikini to do your chores, you are inviting monkey business. But *seriously,* ladies . . .

When you phone your local repair service, say exactly what you want or think you need to have done and ask for a rough estimate of price. When the repairman arrives, there's no need to be wearing your Bill Blass best but do be well covered and no bathrobes, please!

Don't be vague about what has gone wrong.

Don't say you don't know anything about machines, drains, and so on.

The British monarchy allows certain purveyors of goods and services to advertise, "By Appointment To Her Majesty, Queen Elizabeth II." She's a working mother of four with a full schedule and a lot of responsibility. She doesn't put up with poor service. Neither should you.

The Ladies Mafia

It's eight days and nine nights since Al called her a cross-eyed bitch and slammed out of the house. Lynne stares at a prune yogurt, her eyes dripping hurty tears, her nose a blob of raw liver, gut acid burning holes in her poor, sad belly.

The phone rings.

"Hello?" Is it Al?

"Hello, Lynne." Not Al.

"Oh, hi, Steph." It's Stephanie.

"Watcha doin', huh?" What does she think a deserted wife is doing?

"I'm getting dressed to go out with Burt Reynolds." Who else?

"Cool it, Lynne. Come on over to my place."

"I've cried on your shoulder enough."

"That's what friends are for!"

53

With the white gunk you're supposed to put under your eyes on her nose and brave tennis-star sunglasses hiding her eyes, Lynne drags her wracked body over to Stephanie's. "Go on into the living room while I get some ice."

And who is in the living room, also with sprained eyeballs? Yes, dear friends, *Al!* "Oh, Al—"

"Lynne!"

Sly clink of ice cubes from the kitchen. Clutch. Clinch. Off come the glasses. Up comes the music. Fade-out.

Of course, Lynne's soap opera will go on. There will be other crises, other wounds. But this installment, at least, has an up ending because, as Stephanie says, "That's what friends are for."

Not that a woman's women friends should run each other's lives or interfere in basic decisions. What a friend *is* for, as in the above situation, is to take affirmative action when the need is obvious and to give each other emotional and critical support at all times.

Men have traditionally functioned in groups based on sound principles of fellowship and professional back-scratching. While savagely competitive in sports, love, and careers, they have also learned to be savagely loyal to their own. As in the words of the old hymn, which men have understood the value of, *If you get there before I do, just make a little hole and pull me through.*

Female friendships, on the other hand, have customarily in the past developed from circumstances. We made friends with high-school classmates or college roommates and continued the associations from habit. We became friendly with neighbors and shared recipes and worries over coffee cups. We spent a lot of social time with the wives of our husband's friends and business associates with little in common except for the indirect connection through the menfolk.

Happily, as women's horizons have widened, we are learning to form our own small cadres of dependable and reliable friends and associates, the Ladies Mafia, a female mutual-support system and trust society that is also called the Old Girls Network and the Girl Friend Game. It is in essence a reciprocal trade agreement by which the women involved agree to respect and help each other in need—and even more important, to volunteer and trade advice and information that might prove useful.

HOW THE LADIES MAFIA WORKS

Of course, there's no formal organization. You won't find the Ladies Mafia listed in the phone book. The way it evolves is this. Examine your friendships with other women. Decide who has proved trustworthy and generous of spirit and begin to nourish this association. By behaving the same way, you will find yourself part of a worthwhile "club" of women who know they can count on each other.

Playing fair and being loyal are essential. A woman who double-crosses another is not only treacherous but stupid. Excuses and apologies are no good. If other women can't trust you, you're automatically out of the Ladies Mafia.

Your feelings and motives must be genuine. The way Stephanie got Lynne and Al together is a good example. Another woman friend might have sat and commiserated with Lynne and maybe given her a sleeping pill to get a good night's rest. This would have been the easy lip service to friendship, a lot of form but little substance. The Ladies Mafia approach is to do something constructive, not just empty gestures.

When you've come down with a bad cold and can't take the children swimming, the Ladies Mafia friend doesn't sigh and say so long—she takes your kids with her kids to the beach.

When she's having a crowd of twenty for a buffet, you tell her you're bringing an extra dessert or bean salad rather than asking, "Can I do anything?"

When you hear of a job that a friend might be interested in, you tell her at once with all the details possible, rather than saying a month later, "Oh, I thought you were happy where you are."

When a woman in the group is suddenly man-less through death, divorce, or default, it is not a generous act to invite her to a merry evening at home with your husband and children. She does not need to feel like "poor aunt Sophie" in the midst of your domestic bliss. What she does need is to be included in a group going to the local disco or a big barbecue where you make a point of introducing her to new people and include her lovingly in conversations and activities she may be gun-shy about joining.

Another example concerns a newcomer to a Philadelphia suburb, a divorcee who set her sights on Vanessa's husband. Vanessa was paralyzed with anxiety and could only fret. The Ladies Mafia maintained a cordial relationship with the Pirate Lady but deftly refrained from inviting her to their houses and made excuses for declining her invitations.

Since this cut off any possible way for her to "accidentally" meet her prey, she got the message pretty fast. Her next move was to be seen at the local diner and supermarket with a man of her own! Unlike the better-known mafia, the Ladies Mafia holds no grudges, seeks no revenge. Soon, she was being included in activities. Having learned her lesson, she most likely will soon be a respected and functioning member of the group.

THE LADIES MAFIA ON THE JOB

With more women going to work, the Ladies Mafia is essential to success. As you move up in a large organization, do what men have always done. Introduce your qualified friends into the company. They will, in the best sense, "owe" you a favor and will work well with you, especially under pressure.

"But isn't that sneaky?" Sally Jo, a plant manager protests. Not at all. Most group endeavors are a form of patronage. Political parties, civic organizations, corporations, all are built on joint efforts to achieve certain goals.

Working as a team can be difficult for a woman who has been conditioned to work and function only for others. Should you hear about an opening in your company that a friend of yours can fill, do two things. Tell her about it. Pave the way with your employer. And don't apologize or overexplain to your employer. Don't say, "I have this friend and I'm not sure if she's right for the job but maybe . . ." Do say, "I have a friend who may have just the right qualifications. May I ask her to call you for an appointment." If you have difficulty saying this in person, you might put it in writing in a brief memo.

Surveys have shown that many women have problems working with people they don't "like." By having the emotional support of the women you do like and trust, you can better deal with your emotions in your working life.
life.

"How can two people who hate each other work together and

pretend to get along? Isn't that hypocritical?" Jody, a newly promoted administrative assistant wants to know.

The answer lies in the realities of survival in the cold, cruel world. On a global level, nations and peoples who don't much like each other must strive for ways to coexist to achieve a better life for all concerned. They use the tools of diplomacy and the rituals of etiquette to smooth over their animosity.

Your company may not be the United Nations, but it is often a forum of conflicting groups and personalities. The best favor you can do yourself as a woman is to ignore personal animosities in favor of team goals. The success of the group will of course include you.

THINGS YOUR BEST FRIEND MIGHT HESITATE TO TELL YOU

Barbara-Ann cut her hair too short. You've got to tell her, as shattering as it might be. Otherwise, when it starts growing out, she's likely to take your enthusiasm to heart and cut it short again.

Patsy's cooking could cause famine. She persists in concocting rare and inedible feasts. She is embarrassing herself. Her husband is afraid to say anything but has stopped bringing business associates home to a meal. Tell her and offer to give lessons on simpler fare.

Tina's children are bullies. Everyone "loves" her and is afraid to bring the subject up. Suggest ways in which several friends can make her boys feel loved and what she would prefer you do if they act up in your house, that is, slap them on the behind, phone her at once, give them a lecture and send them home.

The Ladies Mafia makes you feel good about being a woman. It provides solidarity among you and others. It gives you a taste of power and a structure in which to learn how mutual assistance creates a power base.

It's encouraging to know you are not alone. Whatever is going on in your life—from the sublime to the insidious—the Ladies Mafia is your army reserve ready to mobilize at a moment's need.

10

Discover how sexy you really are

Sexiness is more than mere coupling. It's an overall response to the world in general and to men in particular. Your sexual attitudes can provide a revealing portrait of you as a woman and a lover.

To discover how sexy you really are, here is a lighthearted quiz that's fun to try and may tell you a lot about yourself. Check off one answer to each question. (If you don't agree with any of the answers, check the one with which you disagree least.)

1. That slinky fur you've been lusting for is finally yours. After picking it up from the furrier, the first thing you do is:
   a. buy a special padded hanger to protect its shape
   b. phone your nine best friends with the envy-making news

   c. rush home, strip naked, and wrap the coat sensuously around your bare body

2. Your beloved has phoned unexpectedly to say he'll be home in ten minutes. You:
   ✓ a. take out the ice cubes
   b. straighten up the living room
   c. send the kids to the movies and put a pink bulb in the bed lamp

3. Which of the following best matches your food preference?
   ✓ a. icy-cold melon
   b. creamy mashed potatoes
   c. pepperoni pizza

4. A beautiful teenage model announces her engagement to a man of fifty. Your instant reaction is:
   ✓ a. she must be out of her mind
   b. he must be a great lover
   c. he must be very rich

5. Taking a romantic drive along a secluded river road, you and your love pull into a quiet glade. You:
   a. kick off your shoes and go wading
   b. recite poetry out loud
   ✓ c. throw your arms around him in abandon

6. You've cooked a gourmet feast for two but all he wants to consume is you. You:
   ✓ a. insist on eating first
   b. give in to his appetites but your mind is in the kitchen
   c. feel "better bed than fed" and let the souffle fall where it may

7. An attractive stranger undresses you with his eyes. You feel:

✓ a. pleased but guilty about liking it

   b. raped and soiled

   c. all syrupy and terrific

8. By some miracle of fantasy, you can change places with someone for six months. You would choose to be:

✓ a. a princess like Grace or Anne

   b. a movie star like Ann-Margret

   c. a movie star like Diane Keaton

9. Which fabric pleases you most?

   a. chiffon

   b. denim

✓ c. velvet

10. Away from home, you meet a man who turns your thermostat high. He says, "Let's get out of here." You:

   a. resist temptation and refuse even though you'd rather not

✓ b. leave with him

   c. suggest a quiet lunch the next day

11. Of the following, what most turns you on about a man's appearance?

   a. a two-day beard

✓ b. his smile

   c. the shape of his hands

12. Of movies about love in the past few years, you most identified with:

✓ a. *Turning Point*

   b. *An Unmarried Woman*

   c. *The Other Side of Midnight*

13. When your man gives you a gift, you prefer:

   a. a check so you can choose what you want

   b. sexy underwear

✓ c. something intimate to share like champagne or a night in a hotel suite

14. You hear about this mother of three who runs away with a lifeguard ten years her junior and you:

    a. envy that kind of all-encompassing passion

    ✓b. wish you had the nerve to get together with a younger man you have found attractive

    c. find the older woman/younger man situation ugly and beyond comprehension

15. About flirting at parties:

    a. if you're with your husband, you don't make him edgy by playing party games

    ✓b. for you, flirting is like champagne—it gives sparkle to your eyes and a glow to your complexion

    c. flirting makes you uneasy, especially when you have no intention of following through

16. You feel most empathy with this romantic heroine:

    a. Jane Eyre

    b. Emma Bovary

    ✓c. Scarlett O'Hara

17. You find books like *The Joy of Sex*

    a. fascinating but embarrassing

    b. funny

    ✓c. a little intimidating

18. You find yourself passionately attracted to a man despite the fact that he's everything you hate. You:

    a. see him despite yourself

    ✓b. stay away from him (despite your attraction)

    c. wear yourself out sexually with someone else

19. You choose your clothes, makeup, and hairstyle to please:

    a. men

    b. other women
 ✓ c. yourself
20. Your favorite color grouping is:
    a. beige-brown-black
 ✓ b. yellow-blue-green
    c. orange-purple-red
21. With a sultry nod to Rex Reed, do you sleep:
    a. in the nude
 ✓ b. in old-fashioned nighties
    c. in "baby dolls"
22. He is kissing you and smoking a cigarette at the same
    time. You:
    a. are worried about burning a hole in the upholstery
    b. are worried about burning a hole in *your* upholstery (or
       setting fire to your hair)
 ✓ c. hate competing with tobacco
23. You're telling him a bedtime story about something funny
    that happened to you. Just as you reach the punch line, he
    pounces. You:
 ✓ a. are happy to substitute grabbing for gabbing
    b. are hurt because he obviously wasn't listening to your
       story
    c. are thrilled that his passion was overwhelming

SCORING DIAGRAM

Here are the *point values* for the answers to our 23 questions. Circle the point score you earned for each question, then add up your point total.

1	**1.**	a=1	b=2	c=3
3	**2.**	a=3	b=1	c=2
3	**3.**	a=3	b=1	c=2
1	**4.**	a=1	b=3	c=2
1	**5.**	a=3	b=2	c=1
2	**6.**	a=2	b=1	c=3
2	**7.**	a=2	b=1	c=3
1	**8.**	a=1	b=3	c=2
3	**9.**	a=1	b=2	c=3
3	**10.**	a=2	b=3	c=1
2	**11.**	a=3	b=2	c=1
1	**12.**	a=1	b=2	c=3
3	**13.**	a=2	b=1	c=3
2	**14.**	a=3	b=2	c=1
3	**15.**	a=1	b=3	c=2
3	**16.**	a=1	b=2	c=3
1	**17.**	a=2	b=3	c=1
3	**18.**	a=1	b=3	c=2
2	**19.**	a=3	b=1	c=2
1	**20.**	a=2	b=1	c=3
2	**21.**	a=3	b=2	c=1
1	**22.**	a=2	b=3	c=1
3	**23.**	a=3	b=1	c=2

HOW SEXY ARE YOU?

If your score is 23 to 34: Clearly, your head rules your heart and other basic organs; you need to be overwhelmed by passion before you can allow yourself to be carried away by it. You enjoy sex in its own time and place—unless you throw all caution to the winds and have a bit too much champagne. While you may not be passion's plaything, you have the satisfaction of knowing that when you do erupt, you're volcanic!

If your score is 35 to 46: You are a curious contradiction, sometimes the wanton, sometimes the ice goddess, a creature of sudden changes of mood and desire. Although you are at times seized by strong sexual attractions, you also have a deep emotional resistance to the sex act—your early training may make you feel a little bit ashamed. You'll find your best relationship with a man who can accept your hot-and-cold temperament.

If your score is 47 to 58: You are a sexual animal in the best sense. You like your body and enjoy the pleasure it gives you—and the man or men you love. Because you feel sexually confident, you can be compassionate and understanding with your mate—and can cope with sexual problems that crop up socially or at work.

If your score is 59 to 69: You'd better re-decorate with asbestos; you're too hot to handle! All kidding aside, if you seriously achieved this score, you're swinging your pendulum to the extremes of sexual emancipation, leaving scant time or energies for equally gratifying pursuits—such as getting a job promotion or planning a family trip to Europe.

Men friends: to have or have not

It was lunchtime. Joan ran a brush through her hair before dashing across the road to the Steak House where Paul sat waiting for her in a back booth. Joan and Paul are married—but, as the song says, "not to each other."

"We're just good friends," Joan explains. "Why shouldn't we have lunch together? We're right out in public where anyone can see us. We have nothing to hide. What's wrong with being friends?"

Can a married woman be "just friends" with men other than her husband, especially if the other men are attractive and appear to be more than "just friends"?

This is a loaded question. To say arbitrarily "yes" or positively "no" is to ignore the realities of contemporary life. You will meet men whose interests are different from your husband's. You will

67

be spending time with men whose knowledge or opinions stimulate your own intellectual development. You will find certain men more reliable or intuitive in certain situations than your most trusted women friends.

As many women re-structure their lives to include career, home, husband, and children, the value of male friendships is increasingly recognized as part of an expanding life-style. How you handle these friendships depends on several things. How you perceive yourself as the "woman friend" of these men. How you establish the ground rules of the friendship. How you get them to treat you as you want to be treated. And, of course, how you integrate these friendships into your home and work relationships.

First and foremost, be candid in your own mind as to what you expect from such a friendship. It may be a shared interest such as jogging or American history. It may be an easy companionship with someone simpatico, a person with whom you can easily talk and explore feelings and attitudes. It may be a man of totally different origins or experience who is just plain fascinating or fun to be with—because he collects Scott Joplin records or tells hilarious jokes.

It may be a much older man—or a much younger man.

Of women surveyed, the most common basis of friendship is the shared interest, avoiding or ignoring sexual overtones. "I need the conversation and companionship more than extramarital sex," Shirley, a mother of two, confides. "My sex life at home is fine. What I like about Lew is his curiosity. We've gone to pet shops to look at rare fish. We've gone bowling at lunchtime. He heard about an old pier where amateur musicians play—it was wonderful, but it stops right there!"

Another case in point is Clarice. Married for eight years, mother of two, she recently returned to work. "A man in my department and I started to drift together at lunchtime. Soon, I was helping him pick out his son's graduation gift and he was taking me roller skating after work with a bunch of his friends. This didn't keep me from getting home in time to fix dinner—and to my mind it was no different from my husband's habit of stopping off for a cocktail with his work friends."

♡ **THE JEALOUS HUSBAND** There was no question of romance. Yet, Clarice's husband became moody and resentful. "I realized that he had not yet made the adjustment to my new relationship. He was miserable and I did not want him to be miserable." What Clarice did was to cool her outside friendships—for the time being. Sensitive to her husband's sensitivity, she opted for gradual education of her husband. "Once he calmed down and accepted the fact that I was neither going to leave him nor have a clandestine affair, I again began to develop other friendships and now he is able to deal with them."

Diane, a skilled banjo player, joined a local folk group and was soon playing duets with a guitar player named Hank. Diane's husband accused her of having an affair. At first furious with his lack of trust, she learned he was taking a ribbing from his friends. Her solution was to buy her husband a guitar for his birthday and get Hank to teach him the basic chords. Now her husband is part of the folk group, too, and has no objection when Diane and Hank "play" together.

A surprising number of women select younger men for friendships. Sue takes long walks with Jerry, eight years her junior. Trish swims with the club lifeguard and often takes a drive with him. Betsy and her neighbor's son, Craig, enjoy horseback riding and spend hours talking horses.

Without "robbing the cradle," a friendship with a younger man can be very rewarding. Instead of the traditional deference to a man's superior wisdom, the woman experiences the enjoyable opportunity of being the one with experience to share and advice to give.

"Not that you can't learn a lot and have fun, too!" Wanda, "a ripe old thirty-two," commented about her friend, Will, a college senior. "I didn't know a thing about motorcycles, philosophy, or New Orleans jazz until I met him."

Is it possible to be in love with your husband and still enjoy your friendships with other men? Cindy, an advertising agency trainee, is doing just that. While taking a night course in photography to help further her career, she met Victor, also married. On several Saturdays, she and Victor have taken field trips to take pictures for their school assignment.

"I had originally asked my husband to go out 'shooting' with me, but he prefers golf. So I asked Victor to pick me up at the house and I even took my daughter with us—I think it's good for her to know that there are lots of kinds of friendship."

The first few meetings between her husband and Victor were less than cordial, but they soon relaxed and began to develop their own friendship. Then, like a Walter Matthau comedy, Victor's wife drove up with him one Saturday with a look on her face that said she expected to find Cindy in a negligee.

"She looked real embarrassed when my husband and I welcomed her!" Months later, Victor and Cindy are still "picture pals." Their mates know all about it. Everything and every*one* is relaxed.

♡ **CAN IT WORK FOR YOU?**   To combine marriage, family responsibilities, and work is a tall order for any woman. Whether to have outside male friendships as well is a question you must examine and decide for yourself. The following questions may help to crystallize your feelings and reach some personal conclusions.

1. Am I honest with myself as to what I want from a friendship with a man? Is it companionship? Sex? Both? Or simply curiosity or boredom?

2. Is my husband and/or family upset, jealous, or feeling rejected by my outside friendships? And am I able to deal positively and constructively with the situation?

3. Am I being honorable with my new men friends—being straightforward as to what they can expect from my friendship? Or am I being a tease, which can be exciting but can lead to more trouble than I care to have?

4. Have I as yet achieved the poise and self-confidence as a woman to fulfill my various roles and yet make time and have room in my life for men friends?

5. Do I have the emotional maturity to maintain deep personal ties with my husband and family and still have the energy for shared feelings with another man?

6. If the friendship includes sex, am I capable of being discreet and have I considered the prospects of what might happen if my husband were to find out? And the chances are that he will!

The office: surviving and succeeding

The way Amy describes it, she had reared her three children until they were big enough to put their elbows on the table without stretching and now she was going to work. "Real work. In a real office. With a real paycheck and real responsibilities. I couldn't wait to get out of the house and be my own boss."

As Amy found out, working in an office is a series of major adjustments. The biggest of these is discovering you are not your own boss. Much as you may have railed against being a full-time homemaker, you are pretty much your own boss at home. You have responsibilities, but you meet them in your own way. If you've overslept, you drive the kids to school with a coat over your nightie. If your hair is an oily floor mop, you wash it and do your chores in rollers and a headscarf. If there's an emergency, you deal with it. However trapped you may feel as a domestic darling, you're actually taking executive responsibility for several lives and facing daily decisions with skill and imagination.

Your home may not be General Motors, but you have been a chief executive. In contrast, the ironic problem facing you as a newcomer to the office world is that you're not the boss any longer. In fact, you may find the hardest adjustment is to such company rules as punching a time clock, observing a strict fifteen-minute coffee break (and having lunch when *they* say so, not when you feel hungry), and following procedures that may seem unnecessary to you.

While there is opportunity, income, and a new world of experience and friendship, the basic situation is that you are no longer just working for the benefit of your immediate family. You are working for one person or a group of people or, more likely in a big company, a vertical snarl of supervisors and department heads who, in turn, are also working for other people (who are working for other people!).

In the office world, your close encounters can range everywhere from the mail room to the boardroom. You may be directly or indirectly involved with all levels of personnel, whose first function is protecting and advancing their own careers. To survive and succeed in an office, it's necessary to get the hang of office politics and to work toward achieving a personal work style that is both admired and respected.

FIRST-DAY-ON-THE-JOB CHECKLIST

It's worse than the first day at school. Or going to a college mixer alone. You can feel the shine on your nose. You're sure there's a black toast crumb in your teeth. Your nail polish is chipping from spontaneous agitation. Everyone is laughing at your clothes . . .

To get through the first day, do all or most (or at least *some*) of the following:

1. Find out where the powder room is. Ask your supervisor (or the personnel officer who hired you) whether there are any company rules about the powder room, whether for instance you're supposed to use it only during morning or afternoon breaks (except for emergencies, of course).

2. Figure out what supplies you need for your work, such as typing paper, stapler, and so on. Make a complete list before filling out the required form. Don't make tiny requests every half hour—that seems scatty and disorganized.

3. If nobody introduces you to those working nearby, introduce yourself the same as you would to a new neighbor. "Hi, I'm Dorry Lee. I've just started working here today."

4. If you don't understand what you're asked to do, say so in a calm, friendly voice. Do not whine or appear overwrought. "I'm sorry. I didn't quite understand what you mean. Did you want me to send copies to everyone—or type fresh letters to all?" Most important, don't spend time doing something you're not sure is right.

5. If you make a mistake, say so, simply and directly. "I'm sorry. I've done this wrong. I left out paragraph three. I'm re-doing it and I'll have it ready as soon as possible."

6. Dress neatly and comfortably. There have been lots of books about the psychological impact of wearing a gray suit and a tailored shirt and whether or not to wear nail

polish and fragrance. Play it safe the first day. Don't try to knock 'em dead. You're liable to intimidate the very people you will want as friends. See what the others are wearing. Judge the company's atmosphere. A conservative insurance company is clearly not the place for a peasant skirt and frizzed hair—whereas a way-out advertising agency is just right.

Some experts say it's a mistake to wear pants at work; you won't be taken seriously. Again, there are no rigid rules. See what the top executive women are wearing. If they're in pants, then you can be, too. Be sure they fit well and are made of a fabric that does not turn into an accordion at the crotch.

7. Don't do your nails at your desk.

8. Be careful of coffee containers. A half empty one that's stained with lip gloss doesn't inspire confidence. Watch out for spills. They can drown a day's work.

9. Say less rather than more. Don't offer any explanations of how you applied for and got the job. Never discuss your salary. If some busybody asks you, say, "I'm happy with what I'm getting."

10. Don't ask nosy questions. If someone appears to take a long lunch hour or have other privileges, it's none of your business.

11. Be prepared to feel a little panicky and frantic the first day. It will pass.

12. Try not to giggle or laugh too loudly. By trying to be friendly or responsive, you may seem overwrought.

OFFICE POLITICS

Once you're settled in, you will slowly find yourself in the web of intrigue, conspiracy, and drama known as Office Politics. As one veteran says, "Keep your ears open and your nose clean." This is particularly sound advice for the newcomer. If factions are forming, you have nothing to gain by taking sides. Stay neutral. Do your work. Don't volunteer an opinion about a situation that doesn't concern you. As for instance, Gwen was listening to two executives argue about where a row of filing cabinets should be set up. "Why not along that wall," she suggested brightly, giving her reasons, which were in fact sound. What she didn't know was that the placing of the filing cabinets was merely a power play between the two executives involved. It wasn't *where* the cabinets were placed but *who* decided it. Both executives turned on her as an interloper.

In such a competitive atmosphere, is it possible to make friends and still succeed? Or must you remain a loner? Office friendships with other women are a refined form of the Ladies Mafia (see page 53), but with one important difference. With an office friendship, you and the other woman or women can be helpful to each other and make life generally more pleasant but—

♡ **DO'S AND DON'TS OF OFFICE FRIENDSHIPS:**

- DO enjoy lunch and coffee breaks with other women.

- DON'T reveal anything about your work or your boss that you don't want repeated elsewhere.

- DO offer to help an office friend in a jam-up of work, though not at the expense of your own. There's a difference between being a chum and being a victim.

- DON'T borrow or lend money.

- DO discuss your family and other personal things in a general way.

- DON'T *ever* let your hair down—no true confessions about either your private life or how you really feel about your boss.

DANGER: MEN AT WORK

There are several kinds of men in most work situations. For your own benefit, keep them all at arm's length. True love can flourish in an office, but it's extremely rare. If you're married, office courting is courting double disaster, because it can destroy your marriage and your career at one and the same time. If you're single, give love a chance to develop slowly and try to keep it *Your Secret.*

If the man is married and you are either/or, you can find yourself in the wrong league. The office Romeo can spot an innocent Juliet like you and soon convince you that yours is a passion of Shakespearean magnitude. It's admittedly hard to resist the professional seducer. You may not want to resist, of course. However, if success is truly your goal, remember that the world may love a lover but the business world doesn't, especially the female of the species.

Unfair but undisputable, the office girl chaser is usually viewed by management with an understanding shrug. The female equivalent is considered a tramp, an incompetent, and—fair game.

"But there's no question of romance," you insist. "Stan and I have been thrown together on a number of projects. We sit around and talk during breaks. Or sometimes take a walk at lunchtime. He's a good guy and I like him."

Fine, so long as you keep your wits about you and that includes information and opinions that he may skillfully get out of you. It is neither paranoid nor your susceptibility to the intrigue of detective stories working overtime for you to consider his possible motive. Think twice or thrice. What you say may be held against you. A promotion might not happen on schedule. Your innocuous male friend may be part of a palace revolution angling to lessen the stature of your department.

On the other hand, as you become more skilled at office politics, you can use office politics to your own advantage. There's no better way to start a rumor than to tell it to a man and beg him "not to tell anyone!"

THE BOSS MAN

A few general words about dealing with your boss:

Define your job. Immediately upon employment, ask your boss exactly what your responsibilities will be. If you are asked to do other things that can be accomplished in your workday, do them without complaints. If additional work means consistently staying late, taking work home, or missing lunchtime, you must make the situation known. Without hostility. Without apologizing. State the facts. "Mr. Fenton, I must speak to you about something important." Face to face, say, "My job has grown too big for one person." Explain why in simple, logical terms, that is, you cannot answer a constantly busy phone and also type complex reports while thumbing through reference books with your big toe.

Women are often—unfairly—accused of asking too many questions "instead of doing their work." How, then, do you find out about things like vacations, sick time, the company formula for promotions and future raises? Not from your immediate boss (who will probably be annoyed from ignorance or from not wanting to be put on the spot). Find out from the personnel department. Have your specific questions ready. Don't give explanations on why you want to know these things. (My husband's vacation is August.) You are entitled to know the facts that concern your job and its future.

When your boss is a man, he may treat you in any of several ways. As a daughter. A waitress. A crying towel. Or a challenge to his macho self-image. Rules of Survival: Do not confide in him. He is not your teddy bear or Dad. Do not let him confide in you. You are not his Shrink Lady (if you were, you could charge forty dollars an hour). This sort of intimacy can boomerang on you. Because you "know too much," he may feel embarrassed when the problem he has confided to you has cleared up. (His wife is *not* going to run away with the tennis coach.) Therefore, your very presence can remind him of his recent weakness and pain—and he may want to get rid of you.

Your confidences, too, give him ammunition against you. "Be careful of Liza," he may joke. "She hates men!"

♡ **PERSONAL ERRANDS AND MAKING THE COFFEE** The two bugaboos of the working woman. Should you or shouldn't you buy his children's Christmas gifts? Should you or shouldn't you make or pour or serve the morning coffee? A distinction should be made between these two questions. Personal Errands are definitely just that, *personal*. You might naively regard the request as a show of confidence in your taste. You might even consider it fun. From a professional standpoint, however, you must decline the honor. With dignity (no apologizing or explaining), say, "I'm sorry. That's not part of my job profile. I'm sure you understand."

Making the coffee, on the other hand, is an on-job activity. If it is for you a symbol of domestic slavery that makes you feel degraded and abused, gradually arrange things differently. If practical, suggest that the chore be rotated among the men and women of the office. If the problem exists just between you and your direct boss ("Mary, would you mind bringing me a cup of coffee?"), then you must take direct action.

"Mr. Dowling, I think you should know that I don't like bringing you your coffee. It makes me feel like a slave. I would prefer that you get your own coffee." He probably won't recognize your feelings unless you tell him. And will probably be very responsive.

On the other hand, if coffee making is not a political or emotional problem, don't make it one. "I enjoy making the coffee," a bright young administrative assistant admits. "Then I know the coffee is good. If you have a slave mentality, it shows no matter what you do. If you're a competent woman, then everyone knows you're a competent woman who makes a hell of a cup of coffee as well as everything else!"

♡ **BEHIND CLOSED DOORS**   As for the Magnificent Macho hiding inside the three-piece suit, your best line of insistence on your own dignity is a bland refusal to play games or get personal.

Situation   He looks you up and down, shaking his head in sincere approval.

He: (Earnestly) I'll bet you look really sexy in a bikini.

You: (Staring at him as if he's dropped a bowl of vanilla ice cream in his lap) The ten o'clock meeting has been changed to eleven.

Situation He puts his arm around you and snaps your bra (possibly with a devilish little grin).

You move briskly away without a giggle or any response that he might misinterpret as flirty. If a firm no-nonsense silence doesn't work, pivot and ram your elbow into his gut while saying softly, "Don't do that again."

Situation He smirks sincerely and puts his hand on your leg or waist in an intimate manner.

He: A girl as smart as you can go places in this company and I can help you.

You: (Removing his hand as if it were a dead mouse) I have every intention of being a success—although I'm not sure this is the place for me. (This puts him on notice. You not only don't need him to help you, but he'd better watch *his* step around you!)

Finally, don't encourage personal attentions from your boss. You may give him the wrong idea and you may give others the wrong idea, too. Don't lunch with him alone in a restaurant. It's okay to sit together in the company cafeteria but don't let him isolate you in a cozy corner. Common in most companies is the office Romeo who romances the newcomer—and then, when he's proven his matinee appeal to the gallery, drops her without explanation.

If your boss says, "Why don't we get away from the office—there's a great Italian restaurant over at the shopping mall," you would be smart to respond with sincere regret. "I'd love to, but—" You have errands, commitments, appointments. Do *not* refer to "What others will say." Your firm refusal to play his game may annoy him, but it can only inspire his respect.

And, lest that sound a little heavy, keep in mind that compromising your standards may get you a good lunch—and inspire his contempt.

Driving you home is another Big Trouble spot. Unless your car crumped out, it's raining razor blades and the last bus has left, *don't let him drive you home.* Co-workers will see you getting into his car (another balm to his macho ego). He may enjoy the rumors his actions cause. Further, he may take your acceptance to mean you're game for any other kind of ride he might have in mind.

Even when the ride home is truly innocent of ulterior motive, it can cause speculation. Then, should you get a raise or a promotion, the Bad Mouth Brigade will sneer that you did it on your back.

IF HE'S A SHE

When your boss is a woman, she may be: Younger Than You. Older. Prettier. Plainer. She may also be an Earth Mother. Dragon Lady. Professional Bitch. Ice Princess. Whichever combinations of the above, she is certain to be ambitious, hardworking, and probably a more difficult psychological adjustment for you to deal with as a woman.

What's more, you may resent taking orders from another woman. Having grown up conditioned to expect men in positions of authority, you may find your emotions reverting to an adolescent rebellion against "mother" telling you what to do.

Keep in mind that your woman boss is fighting her own male-dominated conditioning. She, too, is aware of the problems of *giving* instructions to other women.

Instead of burning up, your best approach is to learn all you can from working for another woman. Since your goal is the same as hers—success—working for a successful woman is literally on-the-job training for your own future.

See how she handles a crisis. Watch her juggle people, work schedules, and the demands of her family life on her career. Learn from her example about office etiquette, procedures, and politics from the woman executive's viewpoint. Examine her career for clues as to the potential for your future in the company.

Yes, your woman boss *might* be a barracuda. Or she may be a discarded mistress of some top executive. Or a psychopath who considers every other woman a threat. But more than likely she's not. She wants to do her job well and earn praise and advancement. If you are a willing and resourceful assistant, she'll be grateful and reasonable to work with.

If she isn't, remember that's *her* problem. Your job is to do your job and learn as much as you can in preparation for the next step. What's more, learn from her errors. When she gets into a bind, analyze what happened and what she might have done instead—and how the problem might have been solved or avoided. All of this is part of your learning experience.

♡ FINAL INNER-OFFICE MEMO TO YOURSELF

- Find the best job you can.

- Do the best job you can.

- Heaven may protect the working girl—the working woman pitches in and helps herself.

PART

YOU VERSUS
THEM

CHAPTER 13

How to ask for what you want

Women have trouble asking for things. At home, we have trouble asking for help with the housework or for someone else to cook the meal because we're going to be late getting home. At work, we have trouble asking for money or for the morning off to attend a child's graduation.

We know what we want; we simply don't know how to ask. "Can't my husband see I'm hassled? Why doesn't he tell me to relax, that he will put the laundry in the machine?" . . . "Personnel told me I'd get a raise after six months. I've been here nearly a year and nobody's said anything." . . . "My mother keeps saying Phil and I should get away together for a second honeymoon, but she never volunteers to baby-sit with the children."

Asking for what you want is a special problem of communication. Nowhere is it more severe than in the area of sexual relations. "Why," we seethe inwardly when the silent messages we send fail to get a response. "Why must I *ask?* Why doesn't he *know* what I want?"

87

Making love is assuredly different from getting help with the housework or an overdue raise, but the lessons to be learned are applicable to other "asking" situations. As you will see, you can get what you want, but you must ask.

LOVE TALK

"Do you love me, Jack?" (Fakey-coy adorableness)

"Of course I love you!" (The cornered warrior caught with his defenses down)

"You never say it!" (The guilt ball forming and about to be thrown)

"Of course I say it!" (The cornered warrior looking desperately for an escape route)

"Well, say it!"

"Rmmmph—"

"It wouldn't hurt you to say it."

"Okay. I love you. Are you satisfied?"

Of course she's not satisfied. Yet, like most women, she lives with a nagging yearning for expressions of affection and tenderness. Knowing her man loves her isn't enough. She wants him to tell her. She wants him to kiss her and hug her a lot and not just as a prelude to sex.

How to "ask" for what you want? Take this all-too-familiar situation just described. Jack's mind is conspicuously not on love. He is reading a trade journal or writing up his expense account or dozing in front of the TV. This is clearly not the time for the Queen Bee to demand honeyed words.

When is the time?

When he *is* being tender. When you've just made love and are cuddled together and he is whispering sweet somethings. That is the time to say (without accusation), "I love it when you tell me these things. You make me feel happy and good about myself when you say I'm beautiful and you love me."

The next morning, when you're about to separate for the workday, you can whisper, "You were wonderful last night, darling," which will remind him of the pleasure that his words as well as his body gave you. Chances are, without further prompting, he will voluntarily say, "I love you."

The same applies to hugging and kissing. A cliche of contemporary marriage is the husband halfway through the front door and the wife pouting, "You forgot to kiss me good-bye." The War of the Good-bye Kiss is rooted, as we all know, in the way boys have traditionally been brought up. The kissing stopped at an early age, condemned as "sissy" or weak. The kissing started again in adolescence and remains, for many men, a literal form of lip service to romance.

How, then, to get that good-bye hug and kiss that you want? Not by flint-eyed reproach. This is one of the times you get by giving. "You look so handsome today," you say. You give him a hug—and a sexy little grope at the same time. You know his sexy places. Pat him on the behind. Run your hand up his leg. Run your finger over his ear. Now, kiss him. "Have a good day," you say, sending him to work titillated and feeling he can wrestle tigers.

Soon, he will be conditioned to this exchange of tenderness and won't be able to start his day without his vitamins, breakfast, and an exchange of kisses with you. Who kisses whom first won't matter. Soon, you'll be delighted to see him making the first move. Not that it matters, so long as you move toward each other.

Asking for what you want in bed follows somewhat the same principle of communication. Save the demands for satisfaction for your five-year guarantee on the stereo. If a man is to be the perfect household sex machine, you still have to know which buttons to push to get the desired performance.

"My wife turned into a traffic cop!" a recently divorced man remembers with some bitterness. "Go here. Go there. Stop. Turn. Slow. Fast. What am I, a robot?"

His former wife sees now that she was wrong. "I was just learning about my own sexuality. Certain things turned me on. The way I asked for them turned him off. After the divorce, the next man in my life told me I made love like I was ordering Chinese food. 'Give me some of this and some of that—!' "

Married again, she has learned to ask for what she wants. "For me, sex is a home movie. I write the scenario and direct the action without my husband realizing it. If it begins to move dramatically, I allow improvisation to take over and then anything can happen."

WRONG WAY/ RIGHT WAY

For any of these suggestions to help, you must first know your man. Men are like snowflakes. They may seem the same, but each is infinitely different. He may be six feet nine and love needlepoint or he may be a bantam with glasses and arms of steel. Take the whole man into account while getting him to do his part.

♡ **EXAMPLE**   You want him to undress you.

• *Wrong Way:* You are quietly preparing for bed as usual. Out of the blue, you say, "How would you like to undress me?" He may leap at the suggestion, but more likely he has been thinking of something else and is merely startled. "Umm. Well—sure—if you want me to." You stand rigid. He fumbles with your straps and snaps. It's hardly a prelude to passion.

- *Right Way:* Same situation. You ask his help with one small thing. "My zipper is stuck," you say. When he unzips your jeans, you say, "Go on—" If he's dense enough to say, "What do you mean?" you explain, "I love having your hands on me. Why don't you undress me?"

♡ **EXAMPLE**   There's a sex technique you'd like to try.

- *Wrong Way:* It's something you've never tried before. It may require certain props, pillows, and positions that are new to your lovemaking. You're frankly hesitant to come right out and say that you want him to lie down like this and put his arm here and his leg there. So what do you do? You try to move him into the new positions nonverbally. Result: confusion, annoyance, and turn-off.

- *Right Way:* You're sitting cozy or lying in bed and the sexual excitement is beginning to build. "There's something I want to show you," you say, opening a *Joy of Sex* type of book. With this method of showing-and-telling him what you want, chances are you will get it and at the same time enrich your sexual relationship.

WHEN RIGHT IS WRONG AND VICE VERSA

It depends on the man. "Touch my breasts" may be the right thing to say to Cal. With Brendan, it might be better to place his hand on your breast and say, "I love you to touch me."

With a man who is secure in his virility, you can say, "Let's make love the entire night!" A less secure man might take the challenge literally and feel inadequate.

As the great American poet John Greenleaf Whittier wrote, ". . . of all sad words of tongue or pen,/ The saddest are these: 'It might have been!' "

A divorced couple were discussing "What went wrong." The wife burst out, "You never squeezed my arm or held my hand—" He seemed stricken. "I wanted to, but I thought you would hate it. You never asked."

CHAPTER 14

Priorities, time . . . putting first things first

Time is more valuable than money. What you spend can never be replaced. In this sense, the way you use your time is even more important than the way you use your money.

To "spend" time well is to get something of value to you. To "waste" time is a matter of personal definition, the judge again being you. How can you tell whether you're wasting precious hours of your life or spending them well?

Your answer is in your Personal Priorities.

You and only you can determine what comes first in your life. Your man. Your home. Your family. Your ambition. Your talents. Your future.

The problem is that most women have allowed other people to set their priorities for them.

Beth recalls, "My mother always told me that being popular was more important than grades." Beth was voted "Most Popular

Senior," married a few months later, and passed up college and the preparation for a medical career that she secretly yearned for.

At thirty, Beth is still married, mother of three—and training to be a nurse. "I got my act together about two years ago. My priorities were topsy-turvy. I was deluding myself that the few hours a week I was spending as a hospital volunteer were all kind of noble and terrific, but I was 'wasting' the time I should have been spending at school so I could become a real nurse!"

Lenore was conditioned to believe that spending time on her physical well-being was somehow wicked, selfish, vain, and immoral. It took a divorce to set her priorities straight.

"The divorce really jerked me around. I took a good hard look at myself. My hair looked like shredded wheat. I had allergies. No pep. A dumpy figure. I was a walking disaster. And it was all my own fault. In all my so-called devotion to home, husband, children, dog, goldfish, and lawn, I had forgotten one person—me. There had never been time for a hair treatment, to do my nails, to go to a health club. I was drinking tons of coffee and eating junk food because it was fast—and how could I take time to prepare good salads just for little old me?"

Little Old Her is remarried and has maintained her changed priorities. A devoted wife and capable homemaker, her private motto is, "I'm entitled to look and feel terrific." She has integrated her own program of diet, exercise, and beauty care into her hectic home schedule. Because she looks and feels so much better, she is about to add a part-time job.

Louise's problem of priorities involves her ambition. Like many working wives, her initial aim was simply to earn some added income for the family bank account. Now, with a promotion and a salary increase, she sees her "job" turning into a "career."

"I wouldn't say that I'm putting my work ahead of my family, but I've learned to be more forthright in using my time. I go to an executive training class two nights a week, leaving my husband in charge of dinner. The other nights, I do my 'homework' with the children while they do theirs. My husband and I have been wanting to buy some new furniture, but I felt I needed a more reliable car than the old heap I had been using—so we bought me a new car."

WHY ARE YOU WASTING YOUR TIME DOING THAT?

How often do women hear that extremely impertinent question? Since it is really a rude question, the answer could well be an equally rude, "None of your damned business," though a more civilized reply is perhaps, "I'm not wasting my time; I'm using it."

It's not wasting time to:

- Spend hours at the library reading up on a subject that interests you even if it has no immediate application.

- Attend a swim or exercise class that makes you feel better.

- Take flute lessons at thirty.

- Let the children wreck the kitchen while teaching them to make apple pie.

- Go through your husband's clothes once a month, sewing on buttons and making repairs.

- Sit on a bench in the park or at the shopping mall, just people watching and passing the time of day.

- Make Halloween costumes for your brood when you could buy them in the dime store.

The list goes on.

Priorities change. An occasional "girl talk" phone conversation can be a relaxing, refreshing, and enjoyable change of pace from the serious concerns of your life. As a daily habit, it becomes a boring time-waster.

However you arrange your priorities, make sure the top priority is your confident determination to get the most and the best out of your short time on this earth.

CHAPTER 15

What kind of impression do you make?

Your product may be good, but if your external packaging doesn't tell your story, you may have a hard time selling yourself. This isn't to recommend a false facade like one of those movie sets with a plasterboard front wall of a mansion and a shack behind.

Nor should you seek to change the basic, real you. This would be like another old movie theme, "living a lie." The problem is presentation. How you take your basic ingredients of skill, talent, energy, and personality and present them with style.

The analogies are endless. The vocalist who knows how to "sell" her song. The hostess who makes cheese and crackers look like a gourmet spread. The committeewoman who somehow makes everyone want to volunteer service and work with her.

There is no all-over "right" impression. You may style yourself

Brash & Aggressive, Quietly Brilliant and Dependable, Squeaky Clean Scrubbed & Bright As a Button, Worldly Wise and Well Traveled, Street Fighter with Plenty of Savvy.

The impression you give is a combination of clothes, grooming, and attitude. All must be related to the realities of your training, experience, and physical appearance. If you're a statuesque brunette with Mediterranean features, you can't pull off a Farrah Fawcett-Majors, but you can borrow some fashion savvy from Sophia Loren. If you are a tiny waiflike creature who has to carry an ID to be served at a bar, it's better business sense to style yourself "up" in more sophisticated clothes—it may be ego-fun to be called "The Kid" but "The Kid" rarely gets grown-up responsibilities.

To help you determine the kind of impression you may be making, here are some basic areas of the—

CAREER-WISE IMPRESSIONS

♡ **HAIR** Is it long, tousled, and in danger of getting snarled in the phone cord? Seductive, yes; CAREER-WISE, no! While it attracts comment, it diverts attention from the rest of you. Your brain power gets lost under your hair power. What to do? Tuck it into a neat French knot by day so you can still let it all hang out at the disco at night; or, have it cut and styled in a new short, bouncy style that says you mean business while also displaying a pretty neck and ears.

Tinted or bleached hair requires ruthless maintenance. In most work situations, somebody will be leaning over you at some time or another. Grim-looking roots do not inspire confidence.

♡ **CLOTHES**   Much has been written by so-called clothing engineers. A career woman, they say, should wear a conservative suit, white blouse, beige hose, colorless polish, and plain pumps (no boots!). The silliness of this kind of rigid thinking is obvious. If you work in an industrial complex in Texas, you will dress differently from a department-store buyer in Chicago. CAREER-WISE, study what the men and women at the top level of your company or profession are wearing. Copy their style at first while gradually evolving your own personalized interpretation. If dress is informal and laid-back, you would seem to be making fun of them by showing up in a tailored suit.

As for the question of pants suits, if the top women executives are wearing them, then you can too, provided you have the figure *and* your outfit is an outfit, not jeans.

Regarding nail polish, boots, eye makeup, jewelry, they must be perfectly integrated into your appearance—or save them for nights and weekends. Nail polish must gleam and never chip. (It should be repaired in the ladies' room, never on the job!) Eye makeup should be minimal for several reasons. It can look bizarre under office lighting. It can run or get muddy in the course of a day. Jewelry is fine so long as it doesn't jingle, clink, or get so heavy you have to take it off.

Necklines, hemlines, and see-throughs tell the work world a lot about you. CAREER-WISE, don't kid yourself that you are only following fashion when you flash your breasts or a thigh's-eye view of your suntan. You will be noticed but in the wrong way. Not only will women resent your appearance but so will the men you turn on. Overt sexiness makes people feel jeopardized. For their own safety, they will avoid you.

♡ **ATTITUDE**   It's a strange psychological fact that everyone's attitude is taken personally by everyone else. How often has a friend greeted you with a frown, your reaction being, "What did I do?" The same kind of responses occur at work. If you look bored, others will think you're bored with them. Also, that you're somehow "superior" to work that is important to them.

Many women have expressed concern about smiling and having a sunny disposition at work. "I'm afraid it makes me appear weak, a pushover," one ambitious young woman admits. There is, of course, a difference between a nervous, frightened puppy smile that begs "Be nice" and a confident welcoming smile that makes others feel appreciated.

It's a mistake to assume a stern no-nonsense mien under the mistaken impression that it makes you look "serious." If you look as if you're going to bite, most people, even the top executives, will steer clear and perhaps even be thinking of ways to seize the first opportunity to get you out of there.

A sunny willingness to help out is a career advantage—provided your help is needed and appropriate. If you indiscriminately offer to help anybody and everybody, you're asking to be abused (and sneered at privately). But when the heat is on and a report has to be got out or some other emergency, that's when you roll your sleeves and pitch in.

Style and dignity are essential to attitude. Whatever you do, do it the best way you know how. The secretary who answers the phone and takes letters efficently is certain to attract the right kind of approval—and advancement to something more interesting and demanding.

Last, but still important, is—posture. How you sit, how you stand, how you walk. This is body language at its most obvious importance. (Did you know that 60 percent of interpersonal communication is through your body language?) Slumping, sprawling, sitting with your legs apart, hardly command confidence.

Think of yourself as a ballerina in a day-long ballet. Choreograph your movements for grace, confidence, and pride, and you will get the respect and attention you should have.

CHAPTER

Confidence tricks

Modern life is a series of tricky situations in which you feel that whatever confidence you had is leaking out as if you were a pricked balloon. Time and again, at work, in a social encounter, while traveling, you find yourself wishing you were The Invisible Woman.

For some women, the problem of confidence stems from having had a man take the active role in most day-to-day dealings. With an increasingly independent life-style, what *do* you do when you're on your own and:

♡ **NOBODY INTRODUCES YOU**   You've arrived alone at a cocktail party or, worse yet, a business meeting. You don't know anybody. Nobody greets you. Panic time. Your knees are melting. Your belly is about to take a dive.

The first thing to do is find your voice and say "Hello" to the nearest living person. Introduce yourself by name, "I'm Eleanor Winston." Don't worry if there's no discernible response. A lot of people are more frightened of strangers than you are. Next, ask a practical question. Where is the host or hostess of the cocktail party? At a business conference, ask for whoever is running the meeting by name.

Find these people and introduce yourself. If there's some bit of information that also gives the listener a subject to piggyback on, do so. "I'm Eleanor Winston. Mr. Kelly asked me to attend this meeting. I'm working on his marketing report." Or, in a more general way, "I'm Eleanor Winston. What a lovely day. . . ."

If this still does not get a warm welcome and you're still standing there wondering what to do next, mildly inquire, "Where is the bar?" or "Shall I sit anywhere?" which will at least give you a place to park your chassis while revving it up for the next stage.

♡ **THE WAITER SERVES THE WRONG DISH** You ordered roast chicken, you got fried. Your guest ordered chef salad and got Nicoise. You want to remedy the situation without making a scene or a fool of yourself. The confidence trick here is an air of *expecting* the mistake to be remedied, your manner suggesting that anything else would be unthinkable.

You: Waiter, this isn't what we ordered. I asked for roast chicken, this is fried chicken. I'm sure you can help fix this.

Waiter: It will take twenty minutes.

This is an old ploy, designed to threaten you with the inconvenience of waiting or to make you feel guilty about wasting food. Call the bluff.

You: "That will be fine."

Nine times out of ten, the fried chicken will appear in a quarter of that time.

Should the waiter give *you* trouble, ask quietly but firmly to see the owner, manager, headwaiter, or whoever's in charge. This tells the waiter you have the confidence of your convictions.

Personalized beauty

What your looks tell the world about you

Like a dusty needle in a record player, many women get "stuck" in one particular beauty groove and keep playing the same tune long after it's worn out.

Ellen, at twenty-nine, still looks like the cheerleader she was at sixteen. Now a competent homemaker, wife and mother who recently started work at a large corporation, she remains the perky, bouncy cutie pie with the pompoms.

Charlene's natural fresh-scrubbed beauty made her a radiant bride. Five years later, she persists in the illusion that she doesn't need makeup, not realizing that the fresh-scrubbed glow is slightly washed out and faded.

106

Trish's thick mane of hair is parted in the middle and flowing past her shoulders as it did at her prom, pretty at the reception desk where she is working but hardly conducive to the promotion she's been hoping to get (and for which she is qualified). Cora once found that blue shadow made her eyes seem bigger; at the office, it looks harsh and theatrical — and frivolous. Peggy's husband loves her in frills, so frills are what she wears while moaning about not being taken seriously.

BEAUTY AS COMMUNICATION

Your appearance is your primary means of communication with others. The way you look is your personal statement of who you are — to the world at large, to your family and friends and to yourself. Your face, your figure, your hair, your fragrance, your clothes, all add up to your personal message that clearly states, "This is who I am. This is how I expect to be treated."

Personalized beauty is not a program of grooming techniques, exercises, health care, diet, and so on. Magazines and newspapers provide excellent expert advice on all areas of self-improvement. The point is that, while you are deciding how to improve your hair, makeup, nails, skin, and figure, you do so within the framework of your own individual look.

Start by looking at yourself in the mirror. Who is this woman staring back at you? If you were seeing her for the first time, what would her appearance "say" about her? If she were a stranger you were seeing for the first time at a party, at a PTA meeting, at work, what would be your candid reaction?

Do you look like an elderly teenager, a child-woman rather

than a woman-woman? Even if your face and figure are still "the same," what you are communicating to the world is: "Treat me like a teenager; don't treat me as the woman I really am."

Would you feel confidence in the abilities of the woman in the mirror? If not, why not? Be as analytical as you would be with a stranger—after all, that's the way most others see you. Women who try this technique often report, "I don't look well coordinated. I don't look as if I care enough about myself." One confessed, "I've been cutting my own hair and it looks it. Squeaky clean isn't enough. I need some professional styling. The woman in the mirror looks faintly apologetic."

Another realized she was hunching over as if trying to be invisible. "I suddenly noticed that my hem was incredibly uneven and my shoes were wrong. I hadn't been taking the time for myself—and what I saw in the mirror was a woman who didn't think she was worth the time!"

Others realized they were communicating the wrong image. "I looked like a cocktail waitress," admitted one woman ruefully. "I was thirty pounds overweight. Seeing this plump marshmallow in the mirror, I found I had very little sympathy and not too much confidence. From then on, it was easy to slim down."

MAKING A PERSONAL STATEMENT

It will take a little while, a period of toil and error, to evolve your own personal statement. Even then, your looks will not remain frozen like a fly in amber. With your own personal philosophy defined, you will also acquire the flexibility to adapt your beauty style to new fashions and new situations.

To evolve your own personal statement, think of yourself as your own press agent. Ask yourself three questions:

1. *What are my best qualities?*
   List them on a piece of paper. Efficiency. Sweetness. Enthusiasm. Intelligence. Good personality. Reliability.
2. *How does my appearance reflect these qualities?*
   Candidly evaluate your own appearance. You won't look like a dynamite up-and-coming success if there's a button missing, roots showing, and a sunsuit masquerading as office attire. Learn to give a clinical eye examination of other women and determine how they communicate desirable traits.
3. *How can my appearance say even more about my inner beauty and worth as a person?*
   Now you are ready for the subtleties of communication. The more sensitive you are to your own inner feelings and reponses, the more "vibrations" you send out. All of us have a hidden warehouse of feelings closed off from the world and from ourselves. Such simple disciplines as jogging, meditation, yoga, and other relaxation exercises put us in closer touch with ourselves and help release all these wonderful aspects of self-awareness.

Improved self-awareness automatically improves your appearance. The more you know about yourself, the easier it is to decide whether you should have red hair, or if blue is your best color (or the color your daddy liked when you were a tot), or if you should give up the contacts and stick with the glasses.

A vital element is sensory perception, literally learning to be aware of your own senses.

COMING TO
YOUR SENSES

Every woman has six senses. Sight. Sound. Taste. Touch. Smell. And—Instinct! Here's how to use all six to enhance your inner awareness and, in turn, your personal appearance.

♡ **SIGHT** Focus your eyes with purpose. Look, really look, at the things you look at, but perhaps don't actually *see*, every day of your life. A beautiful building. The view from the bedroom window. Your man's face when he's asleep. A pair of worn boots. Linger over the details. Take mental pictures and then actual snapshots as extensions of your eyes.

♡ **SOUND** Tune in your ears. Listen, really listen, to the world around you. This includes the medley of children in another room, co-workers having lunch at the next table, a knot of neighbors at the barbecue. Soon you'll hear, not only what they're saying, but what they mean.

As an awareness exercise, close your eyes. You'll be amazed at the variety of sounds you can identify. The hum of the refrigerator, the neighbor's power drill, country music across the way, a stew simmering, your supervisor pouring honey into her phone.

In these instances, you need not hear words to hear meaning. With practice, you can "hear" the voice of your own inner judgment and have the confidence to obey it. With more practice, you can hear "between the lines" of what others are really trying to say about their feelings and attitudes. You can also "hear" what they really wish of you, the sincerity of their voices, and be able to distinguish between genuine feeling and hypocrisy.

♡ **TASTE**   Educate your palate to old and new flavorings, textures, spices, and combinations. Spike the plain yogurt with horse-radish. Chew string beans raw. Freeze some leftover coffee into ice lollies. Add curry to the egg salad. Have onion soup in bed for Sunday morning. Toss bran as a crunchy topping on the vanilla ice cream (with chocolate sauce if you must!).

By opening your mind as well as your mouth to new possibilities, you broaden your potential for enjoyment—and awareness.

♡ **TOUCH**   Feel, really feel, the texture of a child's skin, of a man's beard, of a steering wheel on a cold morning, of hot sand, of a crisp apple—of your love's body and your own. Move on to other tactile pleasures: carpentry, pottery, origami. Build a model car with your child. Take apart a clock and reassemble it.

Gather together a group of "touchings": feather, sponge, fur, nails, marbles, peanuts, golf ball. Close your eyes and feel each one in turn. What do your fingers "see"?

♡ **SMELL**   Listen to your nose as it responds to the wealth of aromas around you. Make note of the scents that excite you or soothe you, those that create anxiety or cause you to feel terrific.

If lemon polish makes you feel luxurious at home, put some on your desk at the office. Flowers, mints, firewood, camphor, coffee, bacon, fresh linen—the list is endless and personal. Try making up your own list and start to let your awareness of scents enrich your life.

Experiment with fragrances just as you do with clothes. What cheers you up on a rainy day? Perhaps the nostalgia of cinnamon cookies redolent of childhood. What makes you feel sultry? Perhaps a man's bath soap as he's preparing for bed. What makes you energetic and rarin' to go? Perhaps the orange you cut into for breakfast or the ink on the morning paper.

♡ **INSTINCT**   Combine all your other senses and add that little extra *something* that comes with experience. Each of us has good instincts. Open your feelings to them. Learn when to trust them. If "something" tells you to double-check for passport and traveler's checks before heading for the airport, do it. Do switch jobs even if everyone says you're crazy—so long as the inner instinctive you says, "Do it!" And when you're passing the thrift shop and something says "Stop!"—that's the day you'll find the fringed piano shawl you've been wanting for years.

In an increasingly mechanized world, there are many obstacles to easy communication between people. Television, cars, automation, and computers improve our lives yet tend to isolate us one from the other. More and more, women recognize the need for closer personal communication. It is up to us to use every aspect of our lives, including our personal presentation, to express who we are and to reach out to others.

CHAPTER 18

The Inept
Reducer

You're not fat, exactly. Your wardrobe is not army tents with holes for the neck and arms. You do not require two seats on the plane. Rather, you are on the soft side of slim with a pound or two too much here, there, and everywhere that counts.

You assure yourself and your mirror that you can get rid of this excess baggage with no trouble at all. The months go by, you've still got your arm in the cookie jar and a chronic case of self-destruction to deal with.

In life's Eternal Slim Game, the Inept Reducer is the woman who never wins because she can't lose. She settles for a fair-to-middle figure instead of a fairest-of-them-all. When the Inept Reducer sails into view, she may cause a mild flurry; with a few pounds less ballast, she could easily stir up a hurricane.

In today's upwardly affluent society, the Inept Reducer qualifies as the new Under-Deprived. She leads a hand-to-mouth existence that can only lead down the Primrose Path to the Fat

113

House. In her inept approach to food, she has Bad Habits and does Dumb Things.

Her hope for salvation is a Slim One. For those willing to stop with the bad habits and quit doing the dumb things, here is the Inept Reducer Plan for Oral Disarmament.

First, find out what kind of an Inept Reducer you are. Here are the ten most frequent types:

♡ **ALICE-IN-HUNGERLAND** Every jar, box, package, and container cries out, "Eat me!" and she does. The original Alice would alternately shrink and swell up. Alice-in-Hungerland only grows bigger. Her Alice chant demands "Jam yesterday, jam tomorrow, and *ever* jam today!" Her life is a perpetual Mad Tea Party as she gobbles everything on the table—while her clothes protest in vain, "No room!"

♡ **MOMMY'S BABY GIRL** Her problem is "Mind over Mother." She swears she'd be lanky and lean if her mother hadn't leaned on her to put some meat on those skinny little bones. Even if she's married with babies of her own, she is a victim of childhood training to consume enormous meals and to give herself "treats" of ice cream and cakes. In moments of stress, fatigue, or loneliness, she allows her baby girl need to lead her straight into the kitchen.

(Baby Girls tend to bring cookies to the office and stash secret supplies of candy bars in the car, desk, and bedside table.)

♡ **THE VEGETABLE FREAK** She knows how important vegetables are, thank you very much. Several days a week, she tucks into a mountain of potatoes, corn, and beans, smothered in gravy, butter, or melted cheese—and eaten with thick slices of healthy corn bread (no preservatives).

♡ **BELINDA BIGBONE** Getting a bit broad in the beam, no slack in the back of the slacks? Not Belinda. She has *big bones.* Anyone can see that. And does.

♡ **SHAKESPEARIE DEARIE** Her favorite is the Macbeth Diet. It starts "Tomorrow and tomorrow . . ." and "then is heard no more . . . full of sound and fury . . . signifying nothing." And losing nothing either in *The Tempest* of eating *As You Like It.*

♡ **THE PUSHOVER** Her taste buds have round heels. She is easily led astray. "Nothing for me thanks"; she says no-no with yes-yes in her eyes. "Well, if you insist—" she wavers even if nobody did insist. "But easy on the whipped cream," she pleads. "And the nuts—" Nuts make her thirsty and that means something nice to sip. Which means finding something to nibble while sipping . . .

♡ **THE FREELOADER** If it's free, she's compelled to eat it, no matter what. Chocolate-covered meatballs, barbecued mule, strange canapes made by the host's son with his chemistry set—if it's food and it's offered to her, she can't say no. With her man, the question soon becomes academic.

♡ **LEFTOVER LULU** Also known as the Walking Garbage Can/Dispenser, she vacuum-cleans the remains on her family table. Bread crusts, chocolate pudding—you leave it, she takes it. Instead of storing it in the refrigerator or stowing it in the refuse, she stuffs it into her own growing warehouse.

♡ **DIET DIANA** Like Diana the Huntress, she chases after new diets with amazing enthusiasm, but is always dissatisfied. The next one will be the prize, she assures herself and all who will listen. She has tried 729 diets in as many days—for about twenty minutes each. The "Stewardess Diet" (or how to unload excess baggage), the "Grim Starvation Diet" (in which she goes out with friends, refusing to eat anything at all until they gang up on her and force-feed her into submission).

♡ **FANTASY FRAN** She lives in a dream world in which the voluptuous Titian woman becomes the new sex symbol. When the wheel turns, she will be ready, belly, hips, and double chin.

Movie producers will seek her out to play opposite Alan Bates and John Travolta while Sissie Spacek gets the ax for being "too thin." A new type of fashion model will emerge, too. Cheryl, Margaux, Lauren, and the others will take up shorthand when this New Full Figure Look comes in. While waiting, Fran feeds her fantasy with—food!

THE INEPT REDUCER PLAN FOR ORAL DISARMAMENT

This is not a diet per se. That's for the Diet Doc.

It is a group of proven techniques for losing weight based on such primitive emotions as Envy, Intimidation, and Hostility. Its success depends on Knowing Your Own Weakness.

♡ **ENVY** Plan to whimper a lot. Cut out the most glorious photographs you can find of the women you would Most Like to Stab. Tape them up in Danger Areas such as inside the refrigerator door. Carry some with you. At the first prospect of Fat Food, look at the pictures. Switch on your Envy-Think. Ask yourself, "Is Cher Bono eating Fat Food? NO!"

A Los Angeles executive and mother of two has the same birthday as Goldie Hawn. She keeps a picture of Goldie in her change purse. When the day's frenzy tempts her to buy a candy bar "for a lift," she dips into her purse for change—and comes up with the picture of Goldie to keep her straight and narrow.

♡ **INTIMIDATION** Masochistic, this one. The idea is to be ruthless and humiliate yourself thin. One way is to buy a new pair of French jeans—a size too small. Don't hide them away. Keep them in sight at all times, draped over the bedroom chair. Try cramming yourself into them every morning and every night. The thought of them will dull your yen for a danish at eleven and French fries at lunch until that hallelujah day when the zip whips over the hips.

A New York model made herself some crayoned signs to stick up in critical areas. One, opposite her bed, shouts, "Hi, Fat Lady!" so she won't do a Midnight Munch with her late-night reading. Another, in the kitchen, warns "Danger! Keep out!" A grotesque picture of a circus fat lady hangs in the bathroom, a frightful reminder as she steps from the shower of WHAT CAN HAPPEN.

♡ **HOSTILITY**   Build up a healthy rage against the Killer Foods that are killing your figure. . . . GRRRRRRR . . . Hiss under your breath, "Fat! . . . Hate! . . . Poison!" Glare at mashed potatoes. Give the evil eye to pastries, gravy, and other Bad Goodies. If, as Kipling said, you can keep your head while those around you are stuffing theirs, you're winning the slimming game.

♡ **THE KAFKA CAPER**   Black humor will help here. You must convince yourself that bread, pasta, desserts, in-between snacks, and sauces have been prohibited by law. If you taste them you will be arrested. Should you see them, regard them as a fiendish trap set up by YOUR ENEMIES in order to GET YOU OUT OF THE WAY. Kafka-esque, too, is the technique for staring fixedly at Forbidden Food. After a few minutes, even a boiled potato begins to look s-t-r-a-n-g-e.

♡ **TASTE SHRINK**   Cauterize those vibrating taste buds with astringent "shrinkers" like grapefruit juice and tea with lemon. Avoid such salivary stimulants as anchovies and peanuts.

♡ **SLY TRICKS**   Love sandwiches? Have sandwiches. Use lettuce or cabbage leaves instead of bread. The crunch is a bonus. Teeth tingling to tussle with something chewy? If carrot sticks and celery stalks don't quite make it, try a heavy rubber band, washed and in the privacy of your own home. It's guaranteed to satisfy the chomping urge. But don't swallow.

♡ **ENEMY DETECTION AND AVOIDANCE** Paranoid, maybe, but it is definitely vital to recognize the enemy and steer clear. Friendly enemies are the worst. Visit gourmet cooks *after* dinner. Avoid street fairs, candy stores, bakeries. Frown at anyone who says, "But I baked these myself!" It feels good to *think*, "Then eat them yourself, Fatso!" while shaking your head no thanks.

When anyone (hostess, relative, friend) cajoles, "But what am I going to do with half a layer cake?" you can get some nourishment by *thinking*, "That's your problem, kiddo. Sit on it."

♡ **ORAL DIVERSIONS** Since the Inept Reducer is a person with an oral fixation, you must find ways to divert your mouth from food to something else. Whistling is good. So is singing. And blowing soap bubbles. Smoking is bad for you.

The best of all is kissing. Why nibble a nougat when you can nuzzle a nearby neck? (Introduce yourself first if you're not kissing close.) Kisses contain no calories and can divert the appetite elsewhere.

Make a deal with your husband for an "I love you" before each meal (maybe he'll even get in the habit).

This one really works!

19

What is personal magnetism?

The world smiles. Everyone is drawn to you. Everything you do is right, bright, and wonderful . . . sometimes! Then, when you think you can't miss . . . boomerang! Your personal magnetism has blown a fuse. You're invisible. What are these mysterious currents of personal appeal? How can you recognize them and use them?

In essence, Personal Magnetism is a nonverbal form of communication. Either you're reaching people or you're not. It does not depend on bone structure, makeup, clothes, wit, wealth, or social standing. It's an indefinable element, an extrasensory "something" that triggers an instant response in people and even things. Suddenly, without really knowing why, you are radiating three things:

Confidence.

Warmth.

And a positive expectation of good things.

119

The new cake bakes as pretty as the picture. The bargain-counter shoes *fit*. The work crisis solves itself. The bus driver smiles. The usual lovemaking merits entry in the *Guinness Book of World Records*.

Why do all the nice things (and the bad things) happen at once? According to an eminent psychologist, our lives are regulated by two sets of "rhythms," one physiological, the other emotional. Our physiological rhythm reflects such routine processes as digestion, sleep, and menstruation. On the emotional side, our "feeling tone" or mood level directly affects our reaction to circumstances and people.

The physical and emotional levels reinforce each other. If your day begins badly, everything else adds to the vicious circle. The benign circle works the same way.

For most of us, there are three stages: *Magnetic*—when you can do no wrong; *Static*—when you go your way and others go theirs: *Boomerang*—when whatever you do zaps you.

On Boomerang days, you're your own worst enemy. Toby's recent experience is typical. She locked herself out of her apartment while getting the mail and had to pay a locksmith twenty dollars. Her shower cap slipped off, drenching her hair ten minutes before an appointment. She waited an hour for her lunch date at a place called Mario's while her date waited at the *other* Mario's across town. At work, she spilled coffee over a twelve-page report. Staggering home late, exhausted and numb, she found forgotten dinner guests waiting on her doorstep.

Since everyone seems to have a personal pattern of magnetism, it might be revealing to keep a daily record on your calendar. Use a star for Magnetic, a check mark for Static, an X to mark days when you are on the spot. After a few months, a pattern will emerge. Maybe you've had five fabulous days followed by three should-have-stayed-in-beds, followed by two uneventfuls and so on. The pattern will be uneven and, like a complex wallpaper design, may not seem to repeat itself until suddenly you perceive where it begins and ends.

Since we're not machines, there are no hard and fast rules about magnetism. However, once you determine your own general pattern, you can take over the world on the good days, protect yourself on the bad days, and find ways to start your motor when it has squeaked to a static standstill.

On Magnetic Days, make decisions. Your thinking is at its clearest and most positive. Do important shopping. Your taste and judgment are superb. Patch up a quarrel. Being confident, you'll have the extra warmth and tact you need. Tackle the ticklish. This is the time for a heart-to-heart with your child, husband, boss, best friend, doctor, lawyer, and noisy neighbor.

This is the time to have your picture taken (you'll look terrific), have your hair styled (the scissors will sing), make a dress, press a duck, stuff a chair, apply for a new job.

On Boomerang Days, keep a low profile. Simplify your life. Lighten your schedule. Postpone commitments where possible. Avoid the unusual. Wear your hair its accustomed way. Use familiar makeup that goes on automatically. Save the startling outfit for when you have the magnetism to carry it off.

In social situations, be the straight man. It's your role to react rather than generate. If you think people are indifferent—or even a bit hostile—you're right. Court comfort on these days. Avoid tight belts and shoes. Double-check your bag for essentials—makeup, keys, money. Keep alert to losing scarves, gloves, umbrellas, and packages. See that there's gas in the car. Double-check the date to be sure you don't neglect an appointment. Go overboard, desert the sinking-ship feeling. Tread water gamely until the tide turns.

Next time you're in a Static phase, think of how you feel on a magnetic day. You may find you can stimulate magnetism by simulating it. When Arlene feels murky, she plays flamenco records. Josephine keeps changing her clothes until she "feels" a tingle of energy beginning to form. Some women find bright colors stimulating. A noted fashion designer responds to pale pastels. (Red, she says, is too much of a shock.) Whatever does it for you, peanut brittle, a cold shower, or "Hey, Jude" played nine times at top volume—use it!

"A good giggle is the best trigger I know," according to Dorothy. She has a mental storehouse of jokes, gags, and reminiscences that never fail to make her laugh. One of her favorites, "I was having a slambang battle royal with my husband. Finally, I yelled, 'You make me sick!' and turned my back on him, wondering what I would do for an encore. There was a pause and then his voice mildly inquired, 'How sick?' "

Are you afraid
of success?

Are you afraid of Success?

Most women are, say the behavioral scientists. With plenty of good reason, they add. Most women have been brought up to be accommodating, pleasing, and supportive. Mother's little helper became the cheerleader "urging" the guys on to *victoree* and later the "good woman" standing behind the Everyman of modern myth, whether to shove him forward or catch him when he falls.

In the great big outside world of commerce, finance, and media arts, women were glamorously depicted as assistants to important men or on important projects. The Girl Friday tag was a glorified secretary and office wife—rarely in the sexual sense but in the sentimental back pat of being the "real" power behind the throne. "Make friends with Terri if you want to see Mr. Big!" is commonly heard.

"I do all the work; he gets all the credit," is the oft-repeated plaint of the female assistant.

123

How then do you step out from the shadows and claim your own place in the sun? Once you establish a power base of your own, your life must assume an entirely new structure. Call it a Success Attitude because that is exactly what will determine how well you deal with people and problems on the job.

A continuing problem *is* people.

SUCCESS SETS YOU APART

If you are promoted, leaving behind other women at your previous level, be prepared for jealousy, sarcasm, and perhaps an idle rumor or two of "how" you moved ahead. You might feel "hurt" that your office friends are spiteful instead of congratulatory.

It's a fact of success that ambition sets you apart. "Everyone" may not like you. Your lunchtime gang may close ranks and exclude you. If they do, they're saving you the trouble of easing away from them. In a large company especially, a new level of responsibility means social changes. Not because you are "better" than they are (although in terms of accomplishment, you are!), but in the usual small talk and gossip, you are no longer one of them. You have moved up a notch to the boss level they are complaining about.

Giving orders is a severe problem for women. One veteran woman executive remembers, "I was in terror of asking anyone to do anything. There I was, sharing an assistant with the man across the hall, afraid to 'demean' her. As a result, I was running to the copying machine myself, typing all my own reports, answering my phone—until I realized what contempt she felt for my cowardice."

Learning exactly how to give orders was, she discovered, her real problem. By observing top executives in action with their staffs, she soon worked out her own methodology. Clarity and calm are imperative, with courtesy making a three-way surefire technique for persuading others to do your bidding.

Clearly state your wishes (with calmness and courtesy).

"I'm going into a meeting. Please answer my phone while I'm away from my desk and take messages. If there is something really urgent, come and tell me."

"This package is due in Houston tomorrow. Please take it to the mail room and see that it is sent by express mail. If there's any problem, let me know."

Harder on the nerves was giving orders to men, even men considerably younger. "A young man fresh out of college was assigned to our department as a general go-fer. The first time I asked him to get me something from the files he told me to do it myself! I was in a panic!"

She, in fact, did get the file herself. The next day, however, she asked him to *return* the material to the files. "Then you'll know where it is the next time we need it," she said coolly. From then on, there was no difficulty.

How you get along with underlings is observed by those on your level and those above. It's the nature of the business world to be continuously tested and challenged. It's no secret that the woman on her way up has a tougher climb than the man.

The executive dining room is traditionally male. So is the executive parking lot. (And the executive washrooms.) Previously all-male conferences are still a tension situation for the female newcomer. It isn't an active male chauvinism so much as a genuine problem of etiquette. Quite simply, many men still don't know how to talk to a woman in a business situation. The all-male camaraderie—which one top woman executive describes as "boys in the playground horsing around"—had to be discarded once women were invited. Replacing it is a stiff self-consciousness and, in some cases, an exaggerated gallantry.

"I know you won't permit me to light your cigarette, but at least let me pull up a more comfortable chair!" a male department head crooned at a recently appointed female counterpart. "My guts told me to watch out for this guy," she later reported. "He was actually making courtesy insulting."

A THREAT TO OTHERS

Success and Power are threatening to others. More so when you're a woman. Your next-door neighbor may comment, "Success is great, if you don't mind sacrificing your children."

Your second cousin Bertha, the one who eats peanut butter out of the jar, may call you "hard-boiled." Your own parents may fret that you're working too hard and neglecting your husband.

Which brings us to one of the most complex problems of a career woman's life. "I had my raise for a month before I could bring myself to tell my husband," a Young Successful admits. "I was afraid he would feel castrated or left behind or green-eyed jealous."

Was it a pleasant surprise when she told him? Did he rush out and buy champagne and put special after-shave behind his ears? "No—he behaved like a bastard! All his own frustrations poured out. He accused me of neglecting him and the kids. He said I was turning into a tough cookie and a few other things I don't care to mention."

He's calmed down since—and apologized. Both of them are

seeing a marriage counselor. Would she give up her career to "save" her marriage? "How can I save it if it isn't there? What if I were to quit work and stay home? I wouldn't be myself. The marriage would be based on wet sand. We'd eventually split up anyway and I'd have to start my career from the bottom."

Lunching recently with a half-dozen successful women, we evolved a set of ten good rules for enjoying success and power:

THE TEN COMMANDMENTS FOR THE SUCCESSFUL WOMAN

- THOU SHALT do thy assigned labors well and make certain that all who should know of it do know of it.

- THOU SHALT make firm decisions in the knowledge that any decision is better than no decision.

- THOU SHALT know thine enemies and keep an eye on them at all times, protecting all borders against intrusion.

- THOU SHALT keep thine own council on matters of importance—for to share secrets is to spread them.

- THOU SHALT set thy sights on the road ahead and figure out several routes to reach thy goal.

- THOU SHALT NOT love thy neighbor even if he looks like Robert Redford—unless neither of you is married.

- THOU SHALT NOT kill somebody else's idea out of hand—good allies are hard to find and thou can always come up with a new idea.

- THOU SHALT NOT covet thy neighbor's corner office —until you know for sure he's quit or been fired.

- THOU SHALT NOT discuss thy marital, sexual, financial, or physical problems with co-workers—because in women a problem may be misconstrued as an obstacle to responsibility.

- THOU SHALT NOT steal Friday afternoons or Monday mornings— until you're president of the company.

Asked whether it was lonely at the top, a woman recently appointed president of her company said, "Loneliness is part of the human condition. I was a lonely child. A lonely wife. Success makes loneliness nicer. Now, instead of making myself a cup of tea, I can push a button and ask my handsome male assistant to bring me one."

She was kidding, of course!?!

Don't let them rain on your parade

Watch out for The Spoiler.

Let's say you've got something to celebrate. It's your fifth wedding anniversary, for instance. The Spoiler reminds you, "Four out of five American marriages end in divorce."

You've been promoted. The Spoiler says, "Every company has a token woman on the executive level."

Your child wins a scholarship. The Spoiler suggests, "It's to compensate for all the time you spend working."

Joys, triumphs, and accomplishments are just cause for personal celebration. You have every right to feel good about feeling good without disclaimer and without letting anyone rain on your parade.

If you are a woman who never hogs the spotlight, you may

129

naively expect it to shine on you at those rare times when your life merits attention. You may be genuinely shocked to find your good news greeted with sarcasm or disinterest.

Because of your usual reticence, you may have "asked" to be ignored or dismissed. A good example of this is Margaret, a no-nonsense fund raiser for her local hospital for many years. One day, the local committee chairman added up some figures and found that Margaret had single-handedly raised more than a half million dollars.

"I think we should honor her at a special dinner," he suggested.

Another committeewoman protested, "It would only embarrass her," as if Margaret herself weren't there.

At this point, Margaret spoke up and thanked the committee chairman for his suggestion. She would be pleased to have a dinner in her honor. She had indeed worked hard and the dinner was both appropriate and an inspiration to others.

The Spoiler is always waiting to cast gloom and doubt. Don't let it happen. Never, through politeness or not wanting to make waves, conspire to your own put-down.

Brenda's paintings have been accepted for a group show. The Spoiler says, "My five-year-old paints better than that."

Brenda should reply, "I hope your five-year-old has better manners than you have."

· Linda's husband's children are coming to visit for Christmas and Linda is thrilled. The Spoiler says, "All kids hate their step-mother."

Linda should reply, "I'm sorry you've had a bad experience. I'm sure ours will work out fine."

Grace is about to start a new job. The Spoiler says, "It's a revolving door there. They have a terrific turnover."

Grace should reply, "I'm sure that's because they've been looking for someone like me."

More and more women are learning to deal with The Spoiler. A New York woman explains, "When I have good news, I say, 'I know you'll be happy for me—' or 'I have some great news to share with you —!' "

Even the clod with the blackest lining would have no option but to join rather than rain on her parade.

Most insidious of all, sometimes you may be your own Spoiler, raining on your own parade. Think about it . . .